PRIVATES ON PARADE

A Play with songs

PETER NICHOLS

D1584706

SAMUEL   FRENCH

LONDON

NEW YORK   TORONTO   SYDNEY   HOLLYWOOD

PRIVATES ON PARADE

First presented by the Royal Shakespeare Company at the Aldwych Theatre, London, on the 17th February 1977, and subsequently at the Piccadilly Theatre, London, on the 2nd February 1978, with the following cast of characters:

Major Giles Flack	Nigel Hawthorne
Acting Captain Terri Dennis	Denis Quilley
Sergeant-Major Reg Drummond	Shaun Curry
Sylvia Morgan	Emma Williams
Flight-Sergeant Kevin Cartwright	Neil McCaul
Corporal Len Bonny	Joe Melia
Lance Corporal Charles Bishop	Tim Wylton
Leading Aircraftman Eric Young-Love	Simon Jones
Private Steven Flowers	Ian Gelder
Lee	Cecil Cheng
Cheng	Eiji Kusuhara

The play directed by **Michael Blakemore**

Music by **Denis King**

Setting by Michael Annals

The action takes place in Singapore and districts of Malaya

Time—1948

THE SET

The sets more or less alternate frontcloth and full stage in the manner of the variety theatre. Lee and Cheng sometimes move furniture and props, to the accompaniment of percussion, thus suggesting the popular Chinese opera.

Over the proscenium, downstage, is a sign-writing screen on which are flashed the names of the various scenes, given in the script.

Steps provide easy access from stalls to stage and musicians are unseen in a pit.

A frontcloth is down as the audience arrives.

MUSICAL NUMBERS

ACT I

S.A.D.U.S.E.A.
The Movie to End Them All
Danke Schon
Western Approaches Ballet
The Little Things We Used To Do
Black Velvet
Better Far than Sitting This Life Out
The Prince of Peace

ACT II

Could You Please Inform Us
Privates on Parade
The Latin American Way
Sunnyside Lane
Sunnyside Lane (reprise)

Enquiries regarding the music should
be addressed to Samuel French Ltd

ACT I

SCENE 1

The Quartermaster's Stores

The frontcloth shows a jungle design with the play's title

The Lights go out and the cloth flies. The stage is bare. For some time there is no light. At last someone strikes a match upstage and comes down by its light. This is Steve Flowers, in khaki drill and beret, shouldering a kit-bag with a bush-hat strung to it. The match burns low and he blows it out. He drops the kit-bag on the floor, waits again, wipes his face with his handkerchief

Steve Anyone home? (*He pauses. No answer*) Hullo? (*He waits again, then shrugs, takes a piece of paper from his tunic pocket and looks at it. He picks up his kit-bag again and makes to go*)

An overhead Light is switched on showing a narrow circle of stage floor

Len Bonny enters from one side, pushing a skip. He is dressed as Steve, but with three stripes. On the skip is a clipboard with papers. Len is by turns aggressive and morose, with a Midlands accent

Steve comes back into the light. Len jumps

Len Where d'you fucking come from?
Steve Bukit Timah, Sarge. Up the Bukit Timah Road.
Len I don't mean where d'you fucking come from in Singapore? I mean what you doing creeping in here like a fucking mouse?
Steve Come to get my arrival chitty cleared.

Len takes Steve's chit, looks at it with some suspicion, forms words with his lips

Len Private Flowers.

Len looks at Steve as if to verify this. He seems a twenty-year-old, untouched, sun-tanned, conscript who speaks with a West Country accent

Clerk special duties. In—tell . . .
Steve Intelligence.

Len looks at him again

Len I can fucking read! Intelligence, eh? You'll be all right here. It's all

fucking long words here. A shower of fucking Einsteins here. Where d'you come from?
Steve Bukit Timah, Sarge. In a gharrie up the Bukit Timah Road.
Len Not in Singapore! In Blighty.
Steve Swindon.
Len Railway junction.
Steve That's it.
Len Railway town. D'you work on the railway?
Steve I came in straight from school. I'm going to be a teacher.
Len You'll be all right here. All la-di-dah round here. And fucking elocution. (*He looks at the chit again*) Demob Group Seventy-Three.
Steve Roll on the boat!
Len Not for you, not yet, sonny boy. You won't be getting no cunting boat for a good while yet.
Steve What's your demob group, Sarge?
Len You don't catch me with no group number. No fucking fear. Regular, me. Five-year tour. Three up, two to go.

Len pulls down a small shelf at the side of the stage, stands behind it, puts the chit on the shelf and issues kit

Right. Better get you cleared. Stripes, sergeants. Khaki drill, pairs two. Everyone here gets three stripes up.
Steve You mean we're all sergeants? Just like that?
Len Temporary, acting, unpaid. Just so we can use the messes when we go away. And all the civvies got some pips up. So don't call me fucking sergeant. Only two of my stripes is substantive.
Steve Right you are, Corporal.
Len No, it's all fucking first names here. So you better call me Len and I'll call you fucking Einstein, all right?

Steve takes the stripes and tries them against his sleeve

Or I could call you Swindon. See how things turn out.

Len ticks the list on the board and goes off

Steve pins the stripes on, looks at them and smiles with pleasure

Steve (*quietly*) Dear Everyone at Fifty-Six, as you see by the top of this letter form, from now on your errant son and heir is to be addressed as *Sergeant* Flowers. Which I take to be a long-overdue recognition of my innate genius.

Len enters with more kit

Len Badges, cap, pairs, one. Incorporating faces, pairs one, face to the left smiling, face to the right browned off.

Steve looks at the badges

Steve They're the tragic and comic masks.
Len The what?

Steve The masks of tragedy and comedy.

Len Get out! Typical, that is. No cunt never tells me nothing. Stores-basher me, always have been, that's my trade, right? I know stock-taking, requisitioning, I know the regulation issue backwards. (*Fast*) Boots, mosquito, jungle-green, soldier's.

Steve See what you mean, Len.

Len Comforters, cap, khaki, other ranks. All right, then all of a sudden I'm posted here and put to handling these cunts: shoes, black-patent, dancing, tap. Type Astaire, Fred. Pairs, one.

Len gives the shoes to Steve then ticks the list. Steve stows the items in his kit-bag. Len produces a cardboard box

Sticks, greasepaint, assorted, six. Putty, nose, portions one. Shadow, eye, jars one. Puffs, powder, other ranks, one. *And* I wasn't put on no course, I had to pick it all up. (*He points to the side*) But what about that lot over there? (*He opens the skip*) How'm I supposed to inventory all this? Tights, fishnet, black, sergeant's. Male oblique female. Brassière sequinned, inflatable, sergeant's. Wigs, auburn, wavy, officers. (*He shows Steve some of the above as he speaks*)

Steve The lady officers?

Len The fucking men. Ain't enough tarts to go round so the men get up in frocks.

Steve Do I get a frock?

Len Only against a proper requisition.

Steve I don't fancy wearing frocks.

Len *Nil desperandum*. It may never happen. You can come here as a concert fucking pianist and end up shovelling shit. Look at me—sparks, chippy, Jack-of-fucking-all-Trades. And I came in as an *accordionist*! You'll be attached to Captain Dennis. I'll take you along there now.

Steve (*shouldering his kit-bag*) What's he like?

Len Terri? Easy-going. San Fairy Fucking Ann. You know, typical civvie.

Terri enters the auditorium

Terri (*from the back of the theatre*) There you are, Leonora! At long last!

SCENE 2

On with the Show

Len Hullo, Terri. We been waiting for you.

Terri Who's your friend?

Len Sergeant Flowers. He's going to be attached to your section.

Terri arrives on stage from the stalls

Terri It sounds heaven.

Terri is sun-tanned, has dyed blond hair, plucked and pencilled eyebrows, matt tan base, wearing pastel-coloured slacks and shirt, smoking a cigarette in a holder. His voice is Shaftesbury Avenue pasted over Lancashire

Sweetie, I can hardly wait to attach you to my section but we're supposed to be rehearsing and let's face it, we've wasted enough time . . .

Len We been waiting for *you*.

Terri You dare speak to an officer like that I'll scream the place down! Go to your post this instant! And you, duckie, I should drop that expensive-looking handbag and find yourself somewhere to sit.

Len goes

Steve drops his kit-bag on the stage

Not here, duckie, this is the stage. Those are the wings, that is the front-of-house, up there are the flies and the whole bag of tricks is known as The Theatre.

Steve moves the kit-bag to one side

And now perhaps young Tom Edison will give us our opening lights. And is everyone ready backstage?

Chorus (*off*) Yes, all ready, etc.

The house Lights come up

Terri It's fabulous!

He goes off, immediately comes back acting. He is a stilted performer, always playing out front, even when speaking to someone on stage

Great heavens, look at this! Rehearsals due and no-one here. I've never seen such amateurs. Dear oh Lord! Are *you* there, Sparks?

Len (*off*) Yes, I'm here, Terri.

Terri Then give me your working lights.

The overhead Light comes on

And take out your house lights.

All the Lights Black-out

Len (*off*) Fucking thing!

The working Lights come on again

In the black-out Kevin has entered: twenty-odd, good-looking, wearing sun-glasses and white shirt, khaki shorts, etc. London accent, awkward actor

Kevin Hullo, Terri . . .

Terri Ah! Someone's condescended to join me. (*To the audience*) Flight-Sergeant Kevin Cartwright, R.A.F.

Kevin Sorry I wasn't here on time. I couldn't find my glasses. And one of them had a drink left in it. .

Terri One of them had a drink—I find that totally outrageous!

Charles comes on; twenty but putting on weight and losing hair, camp but matronly, Yorkshire accent

Charles Sorry I wasn't here on time.
Terri Well, Sergeant Charles Bishop, Royal Army Medical Corps, what's your excuse?
Charles You know how fond I am of music.
Terri Well?
Charles I've been listening to a three-piece orchestra.
Terri Yes?
Charles And the third piece was rather long.
Terri This is too much, honestly! Take your places without another word.

Len comes on. He cannot act at all

Len Sorry I was not here on time.
Terri Never mind, Sergeant Len Bonny, Royal Electrical and Mechanical Engineers, tell me, where've you been?
Len I've been buying my wife a dress.
Terri A dress? That's nice. What kind of a dress?
Len A biblical dress.
Terri A biblical dress? What's that when it's at home?
Len You know—Lo and Behold!
Terri *(with gestures to explain)* Low—and behold?
Len I shall find it hard to look her in the face.
Terri You'll find it hard to look—I refuse to listen to another solitary word.

Eric comes on, twenty, plain, ungainly, hair shaved well above the ears, wearing issue glasses and sweating profusely into K.D. He has a plummy voice and a hearty demotic manner

Who's this? Sergeant Eric Young-Love, R.A.F. You're late for rehearsal.
Eric I've been eating at my girl-friend's.
Terri Is your girl-friend a good cook?
Eric Oh Lord, no! Even the mouse ite eat. Mice eat out!
Terri Oh, Jesus!
Eric I can do it, honestly, Terri . . .
Terri Even Leonora got her lines right.
Len And I didn't come here as an actor. I come as a fucking accordionist.
Terri All right! Carry on. *(He claps his hands for attention)* Well, everyone's here but Sylvia. Where is Sylvia, where is she?

They all pretend to search the stage

Sylvia appears: twenty-eight, Eurasian, beautiful, speaks with an Indian intonation, wears a dress and high-heeled shoes

Sylvia *(joining them looking)* Who are we looking for?
Terri You! Temporary Lieutenant Sylvia Morgan of no fixed abode. Where have you been?

Sylvia I'd rather you didn't say that, Terri.
Terri What—where've you been?
Sylvia Of no fixed abode. It doesn't sound very nice.
Terri It only means you're not in any of the services, duckie.
Sylvia I'm sorry but it makes me sound not entirely respectable.
Terri My dears, the temperament. You'd think it was Drury Lane. Get on!
Sylvia I've been answering an advert for a girl to help in the officers' mess.
Terri Did you get the job?
Sylvia No, they said they wanted a girl who'd been in a mess before.
Terri I will not countenance another word! Are you all ready?
Chorus Yes.
Terri Are you all steady?
Chorus Yes.
Terri Then lights, action, music!

Stage lighting. They line up and band strikes up. They sing their opener

Chorus   What shall we do for an opening number?
                Waltzes are schmaltz and we're sick of the rhumba,
Front Row Crests of the Wave are too hackneyed by far.
Chorus   Hey, what about letting them know who we are?

                We're Sadusea
                And on the other hand we're glad to see
                You've come along tonight to join our laughter,
                To see our dance,
                To feel a touch of magic and a breath of romance.
                We've taken pains
                To see our show's the sort that entertains
                And now there's nothing very much remaining
                Except for naming
                The Company;
                We're Sadusea,
                We're S.A.D.U.S.E.A.,
                Song and Dance Unit South East Asia.

They move about in planned confusion and take individual lines in the next verse

Len What . . .?
Terri Not yet.

Verse:

Chorus   What can we do for the rest of the chorus?
                They know who we are so they know what to call us,
                We're ready and steady and rarin' to go.
                Hey, what about saying the name of the show?

They form a line and sing in unison

                It's Jamboree,
                We're bringing you a Jungle Jamboree.

Len	We've got together in this equatorial latitude,
Chorus	To chase your blues away and change your attitude.
	So now you'll see
	We've got the kind of personality
	To make you come with us upon a spree
	Or a pot-pourri
	Or a jubilee
Terri	So one-two-three for
Chorus	S.A.D.U.S.E.A.
	And their Jingle-Jangle-Jungle Jamboree!

They all dance off as the Lights change.

SCENE 3

Single Men in Barracks

The cloth is flown to reveal a bar-counter with shelves of bottles behind, stools in front. Lee and Cheng, wearing black, place other chairs and a table downstage while Chinese percussion is played. After setting the stage, they bow. Lee goes behind the bar, Cheng stands to one side

Reg Drummond enters. He is tough, good-looking, wearing C.S.M.s insignia. He is followed by Steve, still shouldering his kit-bag

Reg This is the mess.
Steve Very nice.
Reg And I'm the mess steward. Any complaints, any problems let me know. Any cheek from Lee. This is Lee. He number one boy. Sarnt Flowers, he belongee mess now.

Lee polishing glasses, nods,

And this is Cheng, Cheng take Sergeant's kit to bearer, tell him to fix velly good bed chop-chop, or Tuan ask plenty questions. Savvy?

Cheng nods, takes the kit-bag from Steve and goes

Sit down, have a drink.
Steve Well, thanks, Sergeant-Major, I'll have a ginger-beer shandy.
Reg Two large gins, Lee. Plenty big like-so.

They sit at a table, while Lee prepares drinks

You'd better get used to calling me Reg. Who else have you met so far?
Steve Sarnt Bonny gave me my kit, then . . .
Reg Poor old Len. Puggled.
Steve Is he?
Reg Wouldn't *you* be round the bend if they'd posted you direct from Iceland to India? Straight from jackets fleece-lined to nets mosquito? (*He laughs*)

Drinks are served

Cheers.
Steve Cheers.

They drink. Steve coughs on his

Could I have some orange in it? Then I saw Captain Dennis.

Lee serves Steve with orange

Reg What d'you make of Captain Dennis?
Steve He struck me as a bit of a pseudo-intellectual.
Reg *Did* he?
Steve A bit of an eccentric Bohemian, I thought.
Reg Not to mention a bum-boy.
Steve Is he?
Reg A raver.
Steve Is he a homo, then? I'm not sure I've ever met any homos before, not to speak to.
Reg You will here. Queen's Own, that is. The Middlesex Regiment. And if you want my advice you'll give the bum-boys a wide berth. That is, if you don't want to be R.T.U.'d.
Steve R.T.U.'d?
Reg Returned to Unit. Major Flack doesn't like the bum-boys either. He doesn't want his brother-officers saying "hullo there, Giles, how are those bum-boys of yours coming along?" Have another?
Steve I'd like to buy *you* one but till next pay-day I'm a bit . . .
Reg You can start running up a bill now you're a member. Two more, Lee, bookee to Sarnt Flowers. And if you get any trouble with any of them, funny business in the ablutions, admiring your John Thomas, any of that, have a word with me. Deal with them between us, eh?

Lee serves two more drinks and books them

Steve Right-oh, Sarnt-Major.
Reg Reg.
Steve Reg.
Reg Deal with them the same way we used to in the Force.
Steve The force?
Reg The Metropolitan Police. Cheers. Same with the Chinese boys. Or your Indian bearer.
Steve Are they bum-boys as well then?
Reg Stealing I mean. Insubordination. Being late with the dhobi. I got a room on the perimeter, what I call my interrogation room. Haven't I, Lee? You've been there once, haven't you? They don't often go twice, do they, Lee? Tell him what it's like, go on. (*He pushes his cane under Lee's chin*) No windows, no furniture, an old guard-house. White-washed walls. I have them white-washed periodically. I won't have uppity wogs on my patch. Will I, Lee?

Lee returns to the bar

Steve Cheers. (*He drinks. Presenting his arrival chit*) If you'll sign my arrival chitty, I'll be getting on.

Reg drinks. Steve lays the chit on the table before him. Steve finishes his gin, coughs, while Reg slowly looks at his form. Then he sits up and studies Steve

Reg Intelligence.

Steve Attached to the service corps, yes.

Reg Criminal Investigation, by any chance?

Steve No, just routine security stuff. Trying to stop the stores being nicked.

Reg No stores being nicked round here. No loose-wallahs in my bailiwick.

Len and Charles come on. Cheng follows with a case of beer

Len (*sitting at the table*) Fucking foot-rash. Itches to buggery. Shall I take me chapplie off now, Charlie?

Charles Yes, you'd better. Two Tigers, Lee, there's a sweetheart. Cheng, run and get that lotion on our bedside table.

Cheng goes, as Kevin comes on

Len D'you reckon it's tinea this or athlete's foot?

Lee serves drinks

Kevin Tinea's what you get on your knackers.

Len I got it on my knackers and all. I'm fucking covered in gentian violet.

Kevin (*singing*)
> There's a blue ring round my balls
> It's Tinea . . .

Len I thought what you got on your knackers was dhobi itch.

Charles Never mind what it's called. Just remember to change the dressing regularly and let the air get to it.

Cheng returns with bottle of lotion

Charles kneels and applies it to Len's feet

Wear chapplies whenever you can. What's the use me doing a Florence Nightingale if you don't follow instructions?

Reg I'm going. I can't watch this.

Reg moves off unsteadily, lurching into Cheng, who holds him up. Reg wrenches away, forces his cane under Cheng's chin and exits

Charles continues kneeling before Len, who drinks beer

Kevin The wogs and Chinks all see the day approaching when the British go for good. (*To Cheng, at the bar*) Don't you, Sidney? You'll be sorry then, I'll tell you.

Len Ta, Charlie. Just have a lie-down before khana. Don't be long.

Charles I'm coming.

Len goes the same way as Reg. Eric arrives the other way, carrying a large tin cylinder which he dumps noisily on the floor. Charles finishes his beer

Eric Strewth! Pour me a glass of iced water, Johnny. Had to remain under cover till I saw Reg go to the basha. You know what he's like about anything under the counter.

Charles Erica, what are you up to now?

Eric (*pointing a finger*) None of that, Bishop. Nothing queer about me. Anyone says there is gets a bunch of fives. (*He takes out his handkerchief and mops his face, neck, arms, legs. His shirt shows great sweaty patches*)

Charles (*to the others*) What have I said?

Eric My name's Eric. Or Young. Or Love. Or Young-Love hyphenated. But don't give me any of that Erica stuff, all right?

Charles The lady doth protest too much, methinks.

Eric I'm warning you, Bishop.

Kevin What's in the tin?

Eric Lemonade powder.

Kevin Roll on!

Eric Wizard scrounge. (*He takes out a penknife to open the cylinder*) Made a couple of mates in the other ranks' cookhouse. Bang-on skive. All this cost me was a tin of issue cigarettes.

Kevin You flogging it to the wogs, or what?

Eric No fear, matey. I'm drinking it. Well, not all of it. You can have some too.

Charles A tinful? That's enough to keep the whole unit in lemonade for a good twelvemonth.

Kevin We'll all be home by then.

Eric Oh, dash it, look at that, broken my penknife now. Cheap Chinese rubbish. Borrow your screwdriver, Kevin?

Kevin You touch my stuff you get a boot in your marbles.

Eric Steady the buffs. Charles, I know *you've* got a knife.

Charles Wrong again.

Eric (*to Steve*) You, what's-your-name, Steve?

Steve Sorry, not a thing.

Eric (*in a sudden outburst*) Right, I've got your numbers. You've had your ruddy chips. Just come whining to me for lemonade, see what you get. A bunch of fives! (*He picks up the tin, with difficulty, and carries it off to the billet*)

Charles (*following*) Now don't get in a paddy, Love, you know how it aggravates your prickly heat.

Charles and Eric exit

Kevin and Steve watch them go

Kevin Old Charles takes care of all of us. Male nurse, he was.

Steve He looks a bit of a homo.

Kevin Oh, he's raving. But faithful to poor old Len.

Steve Is Len a homo, too? As well as puggled?

Kevin He's easy. He's got a wife in Blighty. But he likes to be looked after. Don't we all?

Steve Not by a bloke.

Kevin You got a bint at home?
Steve Girl I write to.
Kevin Me too. Mine's at school. All love and kisses and current affairs but I have the odd wank over her photo. Funny thing, I've never had a white bint. You?
Steve No.
Kevin Plenty of Chinks, one or two Malays, the odd wog and a few Anglos. But when it comes to white bints, I tuck in my mosquito net and think about Rita Hayworth.
Steve Don't we all!

SCENE 4

Les Girls

Musical introduction. During the song, the CURTAINS *close behind Kevin and Steve*

Kevin   When things are getting kinda tough
             And maybe I feel I've had enough,
             I shut my ears and close my eyes
             And turn on my Technicolor Paradise.
Steve   When the mercury starts to soar
             And I can't keep control any more,
             I study the cinema magazines
             Imagining all those glamour queens.
Both   (*Chorus*)
             In my mind there's a movie show
             Of the kind I can always go
             To find my favourite Hollywood star
             From Esther Williams to Hedy LaMarr.

             Night and day on that silver screen
             Alice Faye can be heard and seen

             And Lena Horne's waiting patiently
             Till Lauren Bacall's had enough of me.
Kevin   Some of them are wrapped in sable.
Steve   Some can hardly move for pearls:
Kevin   Rita Hayworth.
Steve   Betty Grable.
Both   All the world's most glamorous girls.
             Left alone I would stay for good
             In my own private Hollywood
             And I'd never let the curtain fall
             On this million-dollar carnival,
             The movie to end them all!

   Eric and Charles enter and join the singing

Quartet Shady joint, street of sin,
            Silken stockings, old Berlin,

Ich lieberdich, Auf wiedersehen,
Damen und Herren, it's Marlene!

The tabs open on art deco outlines, and drifting smoke. Terri as Dietrich in
"The Blue Angel" is straddling a Bentwood chair

Terri   In a sleazy cabaret
Where the clients were so pally
Once I sang the night away
That's become the Karl Marx Allee
Danke schon, comrades, *danke schon*
I can't run in heels like this
So come on, boys, one last kiss.
Danke schön for *nicht, Kameraden, danke schön.*
Auf Wiedersehen.

The Lights fade to a Black-out

All except Steve exit

A spot comes up on Steve

Steve Dad will, I am convinced, insist on knowing the whys and where-
fores. SADUSEA is a small part of a large transit camp. Each pair of
men shares a room with a balcony, from which one can look down on
the small marquee which is our dining-room, with its adjacent ping-
pong table and piano. As for the personnel of this *outré* establishment,
it has its usual quota of illiterate morons but also quite a few pseudo-
intellectuals. One of these is Captain Dennis, who may be a genius but
it's too early to judge. I will write more tomorrow after seeing him
tonight in the dress-rehearsal of his show at the Garrison Theatre. I
wanted to dash down there first and no doubt erroneous impressions.
Love to you all. Yours, Steve.

Steve goes off as Reg comes on from the other side, furtively. He watches
Steve go, then turns to the audience

Reg They must think I'm a bloody zombie, a moon man. Royal Army
Service Corps? A likely story. Special Investigation Branch if I know
anything. Well, Private Flowers, S.I.B., you'll need to get your knees
very brown to catch me. And I hope wherever they train you spies they
pay attention to your weapon training. You're going to need it.

Reg turns and goes, unsteadily

<h2 style="text-align:center">Scene 5</h2>

Beginners, Please

The tabs part on Terri's dressing-room: there is a table to one side with
electric bulbs round a mirror. Terri as Dietrich is sitting at a table with a glass
of spirit, lighting a cigarette. There is a knock on the door

Terri Come in, if you're pretty.

Steve enters uncertainly, dressed K.D.

Terri looks him over

Quite right. Pretty as a picture.

Steve You told me to come round half-time and you'd clear my chitty.

Terri Sometimes I go too far.

Steve So you could accept me on your strength.

Terri D'you think we've time before "beginners"?

Steve Then you said you were going to think how to use me in the show.

Terri Well, now, let me see. (*He takes off the top hat and puts it on the table, he leaves on the wig; during this scene he changes from this into the uniform of a Royal Naval Rating. It is done in a way to frighten or excite Steve. He pours a glass of gin and gives it to Steve*) Drinkie?

Steve Thanks.

Terri (*pouring another drink*) You see, we're a bit short on the technical side.

Steve I thought Len Bonny did the stage managing?

Terri Leonora can't really cope. She's like my mother in the old folks' home, forever losing her teeth or catching fire to her knickers. We need someone to arrange things, fix meals, the sleeping quarters, see we've got a practical piano. Could you cope?

Steve You mean: could I handle the business end?

Terri (*ogling*) You come right out with it, don't you?

Steve I think I could, yes.

Terri Then, dear heart, you're engaged.

Steve And what should I do in the show?

Terri Well, a bit here, a bit there.

Steve That's all right. I don't expect to hold down any big parts right away.

Terri Few of us are that lucky.

Steve That's part of the job, isn't it? My father's always telling me that.

Terri She knows her onions, then. You'll play as cast, with or without drag. That means wearing frocks.

Steve Mister Dennis, I think it's only fair to warn you I'm not a homosexual.

Terri Don't worry, love, it won't show from the front.

Steve Obviously there are quite a few homosexuals here, which is perfectly all right as far as I'm concerned . . .

Terri Bona for you.

Steve But I'm not at all that way inclined myself.

Terri Oh, I can see. You positively shriek butch from every pore. But then you can't always judge a sausage by its foreskin. Half the rough trade walking about you'd never tell were queens.

Steve Sorry?

Terri Why d'you think they call it the *Royal* Navy? It's all part of life's rich tapestry, ducks, the gay panoply of the passing years. (*By this time he has removed the stockings, suspenders, etc., and the female face but retains the wig. He now stands and takes off the dress, revealing a tanned* *body naked but for bikini briefs. He moves across, passing close to Steve)*

Steve recoils. Terri stares at him

You flatter yourself. No-one's that irresistible.

Steve I was only getting out of your way.

Terri We know what you were doing, Ada. You thought I was after your nuts. (*He hangs the dress on the rail, takes a sailor costume and begins putting it on*) What was your name? Stephanie, didn't you say? Pour me another gin, dear, and have one yourself.

Steve goes to the table and obeys. Terri watches

I bet the future Mrs Flowers can't wait for the day she sees you standing there with your discharge in your hand? Eh? That's better. You've got a *nice* smile, you should use it more often.

Steve There isn't any future Mrs Flowers. Just a pen-friend. A schoolgirl.

Terri So you're not keeping yourself? In that case, I suppose you're down Racecourse Road every night touching up the Taxi Girls . . .

Steve Quite a few of the bods do but I find that such a squalid transaction. Putting love on a commercial basis. Have you read *Mrs Warren's Profession*?

Terri Oh that Bernadette Shaw! What a chatterbox! Nags away from asshole to breakfast-time but never sees what's staring her in the face.

Steve Oh, I couldn't agree with that.

Terri But she never even lost her maidenhead till she was fifty-eight or something. Are *you* a virgin, sweetie?

Steve Me? No! Not really.

Terri (*finishing putting on the bell-bottomed trousers*) You can talk to your auntie, dear. I know what it's like when you're young. The pressure to be a big strong man. I went through all that. My father thought the ultimate in masculinity was to stick your chopper into anything that wore a skirt.

Steve Mine isn't at all like that. In fact, I've never thought of him having sex at all.

Terri I tried not to disappoint my father, much as I disliked her. God knows I tried. I remember as though it was yesterday the first time I got my hand on a girl's tit. In a cinema, it was, in Walthamstow.

Terri takes off the wig and puts on the sweater. Steve sits at the table, facing away, gulping gin and pouring another glass

I'd got my arm round the other side but I found I couldn't do much with that so I started on the near side with the free hand. The first discovery was that it was all soft.

Steve Didn't you know *that*?

Terri I was never quite sure till then that tits didn't have bones. Anyway. Next I twiddled with the nipple for a bit.

Steve Through her dress?

Terri Under her jumper. I'd pulled her bra down on my side.

Steve Did you like it? Twiddling her nipple?

Terri It was a lot like tuning a wireless.

Steve Did *she* like it?

Terri God knows. I looked at her face from time to time but she was staring at the screen as though she was hypnotized. I began to wonder if touching their tits sent them into a coma.

Steve Not as a general rule, no.

Terri Anyway, I sat there holding this great thing in my hand, in agony with pins and needles, but it seemed rude to put it back, so I kept on squeezing and tweaking till suddenly the lights went up and I dropped it like a hot brick.

Steve Didn't she react at all?

Terri She looked at me and said: "That was smashing, I liked the ending, how about getting me a choc-ice?" And while I was queueing up, I thought to myself; Ada, that's strictly not for you. (*Now dressed as a sailor, he moves towards Steve*)

Steve Well, it is for me. If only I knew *how.*

Terri Don't you then?

Steve Well—several times at home I got a woman in my upstairs room— used to get in a hell of a state with ears all red and hair messed up. I could undo their bras all right—got my hand up their skirts once or twice but—what d'you do after *that*?

Terri Are you asking *me*, duckie? I gather you're supposed to titivate the clitoris.

Steve Yes, but where *is* it?

Terri Search me.

Steve When sergeant-majors say: "You'd know it if it had hairs round it," the fact is most of us wouldn't.

Len (*off*) Second half beginners, please.

Terri (*calling*) Merci, blow-through.

Steve I better get back to my seat.

While they talk, Terri signs Steve's form—with eyebrow pencil

Terri Enjoying the dress rehearsal?

Steve I think it'll go down very well.

Terri I get a bit puffed these days. Too many Churchman's, too many choppers. Here. And if I were you, some day soon I'd pick up a Chinese girl in the Happy World. They're professionals, dear, they've even got a union.

Steve Yes, but I feel that physical love must grow from personal affection, there must be——

Terri Leave your name and number, ducks, we'll be in touch.

Steve smiles, makes for the door, he staggers slightly

Ooops.

Steve Not used to all this gin.

Steve exits

Terri checks his appearance in a glass, then turns to the audience. As he speaks the cloth comes down behind him and the Lights fade to a spot

Terri I was like her once upon a time, believe it or not. Romantic, idealistic. Nothing sordid or unforgivable could happen. Nobody could break your heart, nobody could use you or degrade you or steal from you or chuck you off like an old pair of drawers when they'd finished with you. But after one or two had trampled over me on their way up the ladder, I thought to myself, "Ada, you're becoming a soft touch" and from that time I played it for pleasure, never fell in love and rarely got hurt. A short life and a gay one. I had a fabulous time, and let's face it I gave good value. Pretty as paint and witty with it. Then just before the war I fell in love again, this time for keeps. And what did he have to be? A matelot, of course. And what was he on as soon as it started? Atlantic convoys, naturally. And how long was it before the U-boats got him? Just over a year. The next-of-kin were informed, his wife and his mother, but I had to hear it a long time after from someone off the same ship in a gay bar. So—on with the dress rehearsal. *(He calls)* Sylvia?

Sylvia *(off)* Ready!

Terri Well, boys and girls. What you're going to see now is my own dance fantasia dedicated to the memory of all the boys in navy blue who laid down their lives for a better, freer, gayer world. And also to the women and children and the poor old queens who waited for them at home. Thank you.

Terri exits

SCENE 6

Western Approaches

A piano concerto begins, pastiche-Grieg, Rachmaninoff and Gershwin. The cloth goes up

Sylvia stands in a spot, in belted raincoat, headscarf and ballet shoes. Lights on the backcloth represent a stormy sky. Sylvia mimes and dances, signifying by looks at her watch, etc., that she is keeping a rendezvous. The music changes. Kevin enters in a polo-neck sweater, cap and dark trousers. Sylvia backs away but Kevin pursues her and rips off her headscarf. Her long hair falls free. Charles enters from the opposite side, barring Sylvia's exit. He is dressed like Kevin. She runs from the rapists and they throw her about, Apache-style, as light flashes on the backcloth. Terri leaps on as a matelot and saves her. The attackers produce knives but he disarms them and sends them away, one injured

Kevin and Charles exit

The violent music gives way to a lush, melodic theme as they dance their love in full stage lighting, but this is soon interrupted

Reg enters from the audience

Reg (*from the aisle*) Take your coat off!

The dance continues uneasily. Reg claps his hands, standing in the aisle

Take your coat off! What's she wearing a raincoat for?
Terri What's the matter?

The music stops

Reg During the rape Miss Morgan's coat ought to be torn off.
Terri This isn't a strip-tease.
Reg Steady on, Terri. I only said the coat. I want to see the dress under-
neath. This number's gloomy, you need a splash of colour.
Terri But Reggie, dear, this isn't a colourful number. It's meant to be in
muted tones.
Reg The boys up-country want a splash of colour.
Sylvia This is symbolic, don't you see that? I'm not only meant to be a
girl being raped. On an altogether deeper level I represent a fleet of
merchant ships.
Terri I shouldn't bother, duckie . . .
Sylvia Charles and Kevin are U-boats and Terri is the Naval convoy that
beats off their attack. After which he and I continue our vital journey
across the Atlantic. My Lord, I should have thought *anyone* could see
that!
Reg Your ordinary squaddie will see this as a rape.
Terri Regina, dear, I hope you aren't trying to teach your auntie to suck
eggs because I've been in this business all my life . . .
Reg And look where you've finished up.

For once Terri is silenced. Out of it Sylvia speaks

Sylvia You will kindly apologize for that remark.
Reg What did you say? I'll what-did-you-say?
Terri (*to Reg*) You dare shake your handbag at me! An officer and a lady!
Reg Are you giving me bum-boy lip? Are you? (*He staggers towards
Terri*)

Charles and Kevin enter, watching

Sylvia He's been drinking. He can't see straight.
Reg Can't I? I can see you, black as you are. And remember this, I don't
take cheek from the Bombay Welsh.

Sylvia slaps his face

(*raising his hand*) By Christ!
Steve (*off*) Don't you touch her!
Reg Who's that?

Steve enters

Steve You better not.

Reg As you were, sonny. I've already warned you . . .

Steve And I'm warning you. (*He staggers, too*)

Terri She's pissed as well.

Reg One step out of line, you'll be R.T.U.'d.

Steve You people think you can tell the world what to do.

Reg I'll throw the book at you, make no error.

Sylvia Whoever you are, please don't risk trouble.

Steve I don't care. They can't be allowed to tell creative people what to do . . .

Reg All right, soldier, I've cautioned you. Don't imagine being a spy can frighten me. You're Returned to Unit.

Charles He's only just arrived.

Terri Sergeant-Major, I'll say whether Private Flowers is going to stay or not. Don't forget I'm an honorary captain and if there's any more sauce I'll have you on the carpet, though quite honestly I don't fancy it.

Reg You better lock me up. You better put me under close arrest because if you don't I may do something I'll regret. I may strike an honorary captain and that could mean a court-martial.

Terri Oh, come on, give us a kiss and make friends . . .

Reg I mean it! Put me under close arrest.

Terri Jessica Christ. Well, how do I do it?

Reg Get two sergeants to escort me to the guardroom.

Terri Kevin and Charles, arrest the sergeant-major and take him to his quarters . . .

Reg Not them! They can't, they're improperly dressed!

Terri Really! (*Calling*) Eric, Len, come on here!

Eric enters in Scottish costume, kilt, sporran, etc. Len follows in drag—crinoline, powdered wig, etc., with the usual clipboard

Eric I don't think I can make that change in time . . .

Reg D'you call that properly dressed?

Charles Steve's the only one who is.

Eric What's going on?

Reg He's a private. He's not a substantive sergeant.

Terri Have a heart, Reg, where can I find a substantive sergeant at this time of night?

Kevin I'm a substantive flight-sergeant.

Len You're dressed as a fucking U-boat.

Reg There's an enormous transit camp out there, with a sergeant's mess not fifty yards off.

Terri Steven, would you be a dear. Run out and fetch me two properly dressed substantive sergeants . . .

Reg Warrant officers.

Terri Warrant officers, then.

Steve What shall I tell them?

Terri Say we want to arrest our sergeant-major but the only officer's dressed as a sailor and one of the sergeants is in a crinoline and in any case we haven't the faintest idea . . .

Major Giles Flack enters the auditorium. He wears a major's insignia on K.D., carries a walking-stick; he is a spare ascetic man, authoritative, quiet, with the air of an earnest scoutmaster

Giles (*from the aisle*) Thank you, Mister Dennis.
Terri (*peering out*) Who's *that*?
Giles Major Flack.
Reg Company, Commanding Officer on Parade, Company 'shun.

The service personnel obey as best they can

Giles (*coming down the aisle on to the stage*) Stand easy. I'm afraid you've had an uninvited audience for this particular turn . . .
Terri You're always welcome, Major, I've told you . . .
Giles Not me. There's been a huddle of transit camp personnel at every window of the hall.
Reg Sarnt Bonny, detail some men to close the shutters.
Len Sir!
Giles I've already packed them off. But I'm afraid they've seen this sketch or whatever it is you're practising. And most of them found it amusing so I suppose you know what you're doing . . .
Terri This isn't a sketch, Major, only a difference of opinion.
Sylvia Sergeant-Major Drummond wants to see a rape. He says all the boys want to see me being raped and in a rape my raincoat would be torn off.
Terri But this is not a rape, Major, it's a choreographic fantasia.
Reg I only want the coat removed in order to countercheck the wardrobe requisition—*sah*!
Sylvia All right. There! (*She takes off the coat*)

Sylvia runs off, crying. As she goes she drops the coat

Steve picks it up

Terri Satisfied?
Reg No. Where's the dress?
Terri I never asked for a frock for this number, lovie, only a mac and headscarf.
Reg Sarnt, you got that requisition?
Len Sir!

Len provides the clip-board, which Reg shows Giles

Reg Here we are, sir. Dress satin scarlet one, comprising skirts full, one, bodices low-cut, one, Western Approaches Ballet for the use of.
Giles Is that your signature, Mister Dennis?
Terri (*glancing*) Let's face it, if you're going to take us back over every bleeding form we've ever signed! I'm an artiste, not a haberdasher!
Giles Surely it must be clear even to an ar*tiste* that equipment supplied out of public money must be accounted for and having been provided must be deployed to maximum advantage. Whether it's a battleship or a ball-gown. Extravagance is always bad thinking. Signifies luxury. And

we know what luxury leads to: the Russian Revolution—The Fall of
France.

Terri But, Jesus Christ, I didn't ask for the silly frock!

Pause. Giles draws himself up and glances at the men

Giles Neither does being an ar*tiste* justify casual blasphemy. Especially
from someone who might be expected to set his men an example of
respect for his God and king. Let none of us forget we are here on God's
work. (*He now addresses everyone on stage*) We defend a righteous flag
and we bring the news of Christ's mercy to people who have never
known it. Otherwise, what are we? At best unwelcome guests, at worst
unscrupulous invaders.

Charles Oh, yes.

Giles Sarnt-Major, dismiss the company——

Reg Company—shun!

Giles —and parade again tomorrow for further practice.

Reg Sah!

Reg salutes, and Giles returns it

Company, dismiss!

Giles goes first with Reg, then others shuffle off, leaving Terri alone

The cloth comes down as Terri speaks

Terri (*to the audience*) And she swept off with Regina and left me feeling
about this small. Well, it didn't say anything in my contract about
setting an example. There was no work in England, the panto season
was over and life under Clementina Atlee wasn't exactly the Roman
Empire. So I signed on for sun and fun. With never a mention of God
or Georgina the Sixth. And I certainly got what I came for. Singapore,
nineteen forty-eight, and they'd booked me in at Raffles. Antiquated
even then but terribly Somerset Maugham. Only snag, it was out of
bounds to other ranks. Luckily my room had a balcony with an easy
climb from the garden. And most naval ratings are very nimble nipping
up the rigging after weeks afloat doing the Captain Bligh stint. Then, to
a mature woman, how romantic, standing in the moonlight saying
"Matelot, matelot, wherefore art thou, matelot?"

SCENE 7

Get Up Them stairs

*The cloth rises, revealing Terri's dressing-room re-dressed to serve as
Sylvia's. She is sitting at the table, turned from us, wearing a kimono,
nervously smoking*

Terri Backstage I pulled rank and detailed Steve to return Sylvia's mac—
knowing one thing may very well lead to another—generous to a fault.

Steve enters with Sylvia's coat and knocks on Sylvia's door

Sylvia stands

Anyway, the Fleet Club awaited me . . .

Sylvia (*standing*) Who is it?

Steve Private Flowers.

Terri So now she's helped young love to have its fling. 'Tis time your Fairy Queen was on the wing.

Terri entrechats off

Sylvia opens the door

Sylvia Come in.

Steve I've brought your coat, that's all.

She pulls him in, steps out and looks about. He is mystified. She comes in again and turns the key in the lock

Sylvia I wanted to thank you for coming to the rescue of a damsel in distress.

Steve The Philistines must be resisted.

Sylvia (*taking the coat*) I only hope you don't get into hot water. (*She starts to do her face and hair*)

Steve Didn't do much good. He still managed to stop the dress rehearsal.

Sylvia What did you think of the show so far? Isn't Terri terrific?

Steve He gets about very well for his age. But what an outrageous bum-boy!

Sylvia I'd rather you didn't use expressions like that, thank you all the same.

Steve (*embarrassed*) Sorry.

Sylvia (*sitting to put on her stockings and day shoes*) Shall I tell you something? Terri is probably the only man in my whole life to be kind to me without wanting to—use me in some way. I was on my beam-ends when he auditioned me. I don't know how I'd have managed if he hadn't taken me on as his partner.

Steve You're such a brilliant dancer and so graceful and everything I can't believe you're not making a fortune. You would in England. Why don't you go?

Sylvia Just like that? Eight thousand miles? Have you the slightest idea how much that costs? All my life I've wanted to go. Good grief, Mummy and I used to talk by the hour of how we'd go for tea at Lyons' Corner House before taking in a show at Covent Garden.

Steve I've been to the Corner House. They've got a gipsy orchestra.

Sylvia Who doesn't know *that*?

Steve How d'you know if you've never been?

Sylvia Daddy told me. He was in the Welsh Fusiliers.

Steve Why didn't he take you then?

Sylvia stands, looks on the rack for a dress and takes it down

Sylvia A chapter of accidents. We were in Calcutta, the regiment had been posted home, everything was packed. Then the war broke out. Daddy was killed soon afterwards in Burma, we lost our married quarters and had to manage on a sergeant's pension.

Steve I was in Calcutta more than a year.

Sylvia I hated it. But none the less Mummy's worst day was when we left to come down here. "It's the wrong direction," she kept saying, "it's further East."

She suddenly takes off her wrap and is in briefs. Steve nervously looks away

Steve I better go.

Sylvia Oh, no, please, don't . . .

Steve I was only detailed to bring your coat . . .

Sylvia I'll play you some music to remind you of England.

She winds up a portable gramophone and puts on a record of "An English Country Garden". She dances to it. Steve watches fascinated

> *Reg approaches outside the door*

Sylvia makes Steve sit at her table and is about to dress when Reg tries the door, then bangs on it. She puts her hand over Steve's mouth, waits. Reg knocks again

Reg Sylvia! You coming?

Sylvia Who's that?

Reg What d'you mean "Who's that?" What's this locked for? Open it up, come on. (*He rattles the door again*)

Sylvia Terri's taking me home tonight.

Reg *Is* he?

Sylvia (*moving towards the door*) Thanks all the same.

Reg waits

Reg Right. Just checking.

Sylvia Thanks. Good night.

> *Reg moves off*

Sylvia hears, then returns to Steve and puts on her dress

Steve I must be getting along now.

Sylvia See me home, please . . .

Steve But you said . . .

Sylvia I've got a whole collection of English records at my flat in town. Do me up at the back.

He does, fumbling. She stops the music

Percy Grainger, Ralph Vaughan Williams, Eric Coates. I'll make you a really nice cup of tea. And I'm pretty sure I've got some biscuits. D'you like Lincoln Creams? (*She takes his hand and kisses it*) A little treat, mm? You pack the portable while I finish dressing.

He packs the gramophone. She puts on her shoes

Steve Why didn't you stay in India?

Sylvia After the British quit? With all those Hindu and Moslem savages killing each other by the millions? Mummy and I were Chapel!

Steve Does she share the flat with you?

Sylvia She passed on a year ago. And now it's the same for me all over again—after they kick the British out of *here*, where shall I go then? Hong Kong?

Steve Who's going to kick us out?

Sylvia The Communists. Or if not them, someone else. Nobody believes in you any more since you surrendered to the Japs.

Steve Don't blame me. I was only twelve at the time.

Now ready, she switches out the dressing lights, listens at the door, unlocks it, goes out of the room and looks about. Steve follows with the gramophone. She locks the door after her, then takes Steve's hand to lead away

Reg appears, stopping their way

Reg Miss Morgan. Lucky I caught you.

Sylvia Why are you always following me? I feel I've got no privacy.

Reg Privacy? That's American, that is. You'd better say "privacy" if you want to pass muster in the Burlington Arcade.

Sylvia Please, Reg . . .

Reg "Privacy"! You been talking to the Yanks again?

Sylvia Don't!

Reg Can't leave them alone, can you?

Reg moves unsteadily towards Sylvia. She flinches, but Reg passes her for Steve

I'll take that, soldier . . .

Steve Captain Dennis . . .

Reg Captain Dennis went off long ago. Full steam ahead to our boys in blue, I expect.

Steve He detailed me to escort Miss Morgan . . .

Sylvia No, it's all right. You must come some other time.

Steve relinquishes the portable to Reg. Sylvia kisses Steve. Reg waits

Sylvia goes with Reg

Steve turns to the audience

Steve Dearest Heather, it is bewildering to discover how many different sorts of people there are and how many different ways they have. It's going to be an enormous task educating them all, even if the teaching profession is bursting with brilliant geniuses like yours truly. If only you could be here for a day so I could show you how little there is in common between Singapore and Fernleaze Crescent. But do keep writing with the news. We all long for the mail to come and you can imagine that the unfortunate wretch who receives no letter is a prey to morbid imaginings and nervous breakdowns. Love and all that, your itinerant but ever-faithful Steve.

The tabs open

  Steve goes

SCENE 8

Forces Sweethearts

Terri, wearing a long white dress and wig, is seated at a desk writing a letter.
On the desk is a lighted candle. On the refrain the men (off) hum to his
singing

Terri (*into a movable microphone standing by the desk*)
      My dearest, I'm writing once again
      From the still of my lonely room
      And dreaming of the moment when
      We'll stand as bride and groom.
      For though today you're oh-so-far away,
      I imagine all we'll do and say.

      When the shadows creep
      Over fields of sheep
      With a love that's deep
      You and I will go to sleep
      Doing all those little things we used to do.

He rises and moves down. The tabs close

      When the chapel bell
      Says "Good night, sleep well"
      To the wishing-well
      And the children's carousel,
      We'll do all those little things we used to do.

      Remember September
      The country week-ends,
      The yearning we felt inside?
      And autumn recalls
      Such wonderful balls,
      The organ at eventide.

      We'll be true until
      In a church that's still
      I shall know the thrill
      Of whispering "I will",
      Then we'll do those little things that we
      Used to do before
      But with roses around the door.

Accompaniment and male chanting goes on through the following speech

  Darling, do you remember V.E. Night and V.J. Night, how we danced and sang in the streets? The bonfires and the crowds? Everyone felt so glad peace was here again and we could all get on with the job of building anew? But in three short years the world is once more torn by strife and that's why boys like you have got to be over there keeping the peace till everyone's come to their senses again. And then, dearest, there'll be so many wonderful things to do together and all the time in the world to do them in.

> Remember December,
> Those Christmases past,
> The mistletoe where we kissed?
> The carols, the tree,
> Your presents to me,
> The stuffing we couldn't resist?

Steve, Kevin, Charles and Eric join in to sing the final stanza

All   On a day new born
        In a field of corn
        There's an April morn
        When we'll welcome in the dawn
        Doing all those little things that we used to do before
        But we'll do them for ever more.

The tabs open to show Steve, Kevin, Charles and Eric preparing to take showers, sitting on a bench with four cubicles behind it. They are wearing only towels round their waists

Len enters, also in a towel, with mail for them

Len Letter for you, Charlie, from Yorkshire. Fucker for me and all from the fucking wife.
Charles Gawd help us. My mother. The voice of doom.

Len gives out the letters as he names them

Len Wimbledon, cop hold of that. One from your young tart.
Eric Bang on, squire.
Len Einstein, fucker for you. Lambeth, there's even a cunt for you.
Kevin I wish there was. A nice white one.

All look at their mail, settle to read and give extracts aloud

Eric This is from Susan all right. Wizard!
Kevin My young lady pen-friend. "Dear Kevin, thank you for the snap you sent. How brown you look! Am I right in saying you are something like Gene Kelly only younger?"
Len "My dear hubby, not much to write about as per usual. Aldershot is much the same and most things rationed still even bread now, it makes you wish old Winnie was back and all parcels very welcome as per usual. . . ."
Eric "You will see from the background of the enclosed snap that New Malden is as beautiful as ever." (*He looks at the snap*) Not only the

background, but Susan in the front. (*He kisses the photo and goes on with the letter*) "The cherry blossom makes you wonder what they mean by a Cold War but Dad says it's all due to the miners not being able to dig enough coal to warm it up, however much they get paid. He keeps us in fits with his jokes."

Len "Do you remember Corporal Pratt that we knew in Iceland?" I remember him, the randy cunt. "He has turned up here, what a small world . . ."

Kevin "When you go swimming do watch out for those man-eating sharks you wrote about in your last. . . ." (*He stops, looking nervously at the others but they are not attending*) Shut up!

Eric "Mum says she can't make out why our boys in the R.A.F. are dropping food on Berlin when it seems only yesterday they were dropping bombs . . ."

Len "Working in the NAAFI is very hard on nylons and I see where you are getting an increment in your overseas allowance. Do let me have a pound or two to buy some clothing coupons on the black market and oblige your loving wife Valerie . . ."

Charles So she can oblige Corporal Pratt, I imagine.

Len You wouldn't fucking knob it. What's your mother got to say?

Charles Auntie May's had a prolapse. Dad's having a stone removed, her feet are playing up. It's more like *The Lancet* than a letter.

Len Johnny!

Cheng enters

Couple of Tigers. Chop-chop.

Kevin Make that three!

Eric I'll have one, squire.

Steve That's five, Cheng.

Cheng exits

Eric Dad says the way to cure your prickly heat is to stand in the pouring rain with no clothes on.

Charles My dear! (*He goes into a cubicle*)

Eric Watch it, Bishop!

Kevin "We are doing Malaya in Geography and I asked Miss why you're out there and she said it was to do with letting Stalin have some rubber." (*He looks up*) That's not right, is it?

Len goes into a cubicle

Steve Listen to what my mate says: "You needn't think you are going to impress people with your uniforms. They couldn't care less. They don't even know there *is* an army in Malaya."

Eric "Your friend Corporal Lawrence hasn't come here yet to deliver the silk for my wedding dress. Princess Elizabeth's marriage set me looking forward to ours all over again . . ."

Kevin Not even sent a photo this time.

Eric Susan has.

Kevin (*taking the snap*) That her?
Eric That's my bit of kaifa, matey, waiting for me in New Malden.
Kevin You'll be all right there. Bit like Deborah Kerr, is she?

Charles comes out of his cubicle: Steve goes in

Eric All right? Is that all? I'll be laughing, mate. In the lifeboat. Asbestos.

Kevin returns the snap, goes into a cubicle. Eric reads on

Kevin You going to know what to do, though? You don't want to disappoint her first time. You come down Racecourse Road one night, let some Chinky tart show you what to do.
Eric No fear. I'm staying clean for Susan. (*He goes into a cubicle*)
Kevin Here's a better idea! How d'you fancy a touch of Black Velvet? Old Sylvia now? She's a good sort. Clever too. They reckon she can smoke a cheroot in her minge.
Len (*coming out*) Blow smoke rings and all, can't she?
Kevin Used to do it in Calcutta, didn't she, for the Yanks? In the cabaret?
Len Takes some fucking muscle control, mind.
Charles You're pathetic, both of you, with your tatty fantasies.
Kevin You want to teach your Susan that.
Eric (*threatening*) Now watch it, Lambeth.
Kevin Go down well in New Malden.
Eric I've warned you . . .
Kevin The Young Conservatives' Garden Party.
Eric (*coming out*) Talk as dirty as you like about half-caste tarts but start on Susan and see what you get . . .
Kevin (*coming out*) What then? What? Come on! What?
Eric (*showing his fist*) A bunch of fives! That's what.
Charles Not again! If Love came to visit you in *hospital*, he'd bring you a bunch of fives.
Eric (*turning on him*) I'll deal with you in a minute, Bishop.

Steve comes out

Kevin grabs his towel and flicks it at Eric's buttocks

Ow! Right, that's it. I've ruddy well warned you, Cartwright, now you're for it—you've had your chips, chiefy, mark my words—hey, steady on, that hurt . . .

The others are all out by now and have towelled and put on their towels

Reg enters, properly dressed, with cap

Reg Company, attention! Officer Commanding!

Giles enters

The men come to attention. Kevin quickly wraps on his towel. Eric is left without, and has to find his in the cubicles. Then he tries to wring it out while Giles waits in silence

Hurry it up, there.

Eric Sah! (*He finds and wraps his towel around him, and comes to attention*)
Giles Carry on, Sarnt-Major.
Reg Last night's guard detail, one pace forward—march!

Eric smartly steps forward, stamping with bare feet

Name, rank and number.
Eric Two-two-three-one-seven-four-seven, Acting-Sergeant Young-Love, sah!
Giles You were on guard duty last night?
Eric Sah!
Giles And do you remember my staff car leaving my quarters some time after midnight?
Eric About two hundred hours, sir, yessir. I saw you coming, lifted the barrier and presented arms. You acknowledged the salute, sir, in the back seat.

Cheng enters with a tray of five drinks which he puts on the bench

Giles No.
Eric Thought you did, sah.
Giles I wasn't in the back seat. I wasn't in the car at all.
Eric Your driver certainly did, sir.
Giles That wasn't my driver, that was a Chinese Communist.
Eric Sah?
Giles He was stealing my car, Sarnt. We cannot say for what reason. It was later found burnt out on the Bukit Timah Road.
Eric I recognized your car, sir, I naturally thought . . .
Reg Can I offer you a drink, sir?
Giles A lemonade, thank you.
Reg Cheng. Two lemonade, chop-chop. Makee from big tin of powder you've got backside of bar. Savvy?

Cheng goes, with the tray

Giles Now I understand the guard for our compound is drawn from transit personnel. So why were you, an acting N.C.O., patrolling our lines?
Eric Volunteer, sah. I've volunteered for permanent Friday night guard duty.
Giles What for?
Eric (*shrugging, attempting pleasantry*) Keeps me out of trouble, sah.
Giles Not on this occasion.
Eric I mean it stops me spending money in the mess, sir, or Singapore. I'm saving all my pay towards my marriage.
Giles I wish you every happiness.
Eric Keep myself very busy, sir, all through my service. Volunteer for everything: fire-fighter, assistant in the early treatment room, clerk to the Catholic padre, dog-shooter, magician, anti-malarial officer . . .
Giles Magician?
Eric In the show, sir.

Giles Ah.

Charles He makes cares disappear.

The men laugh. Giles stiffens

Giles You wouldn't find it quite so funny if the Communists had burnt your billet with you inside. Or lined you and your family up against a wall and sprayed you with machine-gun fire. That's already happening, d'you know that? Not only to British planters but Indian managers, Chinese businessmen, Malayan farmers. Anyone's fair game! As you were. Anyone prepared to save Malaya from a new dark age of atheism. That is what we're here for. And that is why we'll stay.

Cheng enters with two glasses of lemonade

Thanks, boy. Now—though I myself am a life-abstainer, I never object to moderate drinking in others. So finish your beers by joining me in a toast.

The men get their glasses, Reg and Giles the lemonade. Cheng stands waiting

To the defeat of Communism in South-East Asia Command Malaya and Singapore and the victory of Christian enlightenment!

Men (*mumbling*) To the defeat of Communism in South-East Asia Command Malaya and Singapore and the victory of Christian enlightenment.

They all drink

Giles Excellent lemonade. Now some of you may be saying "Yes, that's all very well, but law-luv-a-duck, we're only peace-time conscripts waiting for the boat back to dear old Blighty." And others may say "but cor-stone-the-crows, this is a non-combatant unit after all." But, as we see from last night's episode, we *are* a military target. And if we don't defend ourselves, no-one else will. From now on we're not relying on transit personnel to patrol our perimeter. Mister Drummond's drawn up a roster for the coming months.

Cheng moves about collecting glasses. Giles finishes his drink and returns his glass to him

Singing and dancing's all very well but it won't stop Communist Chinamen. That's all, men.

Reg Company, attention!

The men come to attention. Giles makes to exit but pauses, sniffing the air

Giles Do I smell women's perfume?

Reg There's a distinct suggestion of it, sir.

Giles I hope you're none of you allowing women in these quarters. Strictly out of bounds.

Reg I don't think it's women, sir.

Charles It's mine. I wear it.

Giles Bless my soul. What for?
Charles My part in the show, sir. Female impersonation.
Steve We all do, sir.
Giles You're the new man, aren't you?
Steve Sarnt Flowers, sir.
Giles Settling in?
Steve Yes, thanks very much.
Giles All right. No perfume on guard duty, eh? No mufti either. Properly dressed, fixed bayonets. But—(*to Charles*)—well done, Sergeant. That's the kind of keenness we like to see, isn't it, Mister Drummond?
Reg Company, fall out!

Giles goes

Reg comes straight to the audience. The cloth comes down behind him

Talk about the three monkeys! He's the lot rolled into one. Bum-boys crawling out the woodwork and he doesn't even see. Still. I got rather more pressing problems. Such as what to do about our pet spy from the Special Investigation Branch.

SCENE 9

Harmony Time

The cloth is flown in a Black-out. Kevin, lit by a single torch from beneath, sings to the tune of "Greensleeves". The song is accompanied and lyrically arranged so that only the words are coarse

Kevin   There was a dusky Eurasian maid
             In old Bombay she plied her trade
             And in Calcutta and in Madras
             And by special request up the Khyber Pass

Other torches now light up the faces of Terri, Charles, Len and Eric. They form a male-voice choir

Choir   Black Velvet was full of joy
             For every British soldier boy
             She guaranteed to please
             And the most that it cost you was five rupees.
Len   There came a soldier-boy fully grown
             Who till that moment had held his own.
             And though he'd served on several fronts
             He'd never seen action on ladies once.

At about the third verse, lights come up on Sylvia's room. She and Steve are nude in bed and mime love-making to the continuing music

All   Black Velvet had great allure
             For such a private, so young and pure.

> She took him well in hand
> And showed him the way to the promised land.

Eric   She took off all her seven veils
> And then she told him she came from Wales
> And how she'd seen the Forth Bridge one day
> While gazing out across Tiger Bay

All   Meanwhile she softly read
> The Khamasutra from A to Z
> And after that was done
> They started again at Chapter One.

Choir   She demonstrates the clinging vine
> And quickly taught him the sixty-nine.
> She showed him some of the ways there are
> That a lady can draw on a man's cigar

At the end of the song the choir go off

Steve (*kissing Sylvia's body*) These bruises. Do they still hurt?

Sylvia No, not at all. I'd rather you didn't pass remarks about them.

Steve Was it during a performance you fell?

Sylvia A rehearsal. It's nothing, I tell you.

Steve It's only because I love you, Sylvia, I can't bear to think of you being hurt.

Sylvia *You* love *me*? Come on now, you're pulling my leg.

Steve But I must have told you a dozen times during the last hour how much I love you.

Sylvia But every man says that when he's doing jig-jig.

Steve Does he?

Sylvia Well, doesn't he?

Steve I don't know, it was my first time.

Sylvia Oh, good grief—I thought you were inexperienced, now I feel even more ashamed.

Steve I knew it wasn't your first time.

Sylvia I didn't lead you on, you must admit that.

Steve All these years being frightened to death—all these years I could have been doing it—wasted. If you and I had met in Calcutta we could have started then. We could have been doing it for two years.

Sylvia Steve, have a heart. Anyway, I hated Calcutta. Dirty old men trying to get you to do disgusting things for American soldiers.

Steve What kind of disgusting things?

Sylvia Hell's bells, I don't know. I didn't do them.

Steve No, but some of the bods were talking and they said a woman can smoke a cigar—you know, not in her mouth.

Sylvia I've already told you I don't like suggestive talk. You wouldn't say those things to that girl that's waiting for you at home. That Heather.

Steve She's not waiting for me. She gets a bit lonely and sends the news . . .

Sylvia Lonely? In England? Pulling my leg again! If a person's lonely there, surely they'd go to their club? Surely they'd stroll along the Strand to Pall Mall for a drink in one of the clubs?

Steve In London, yes, but this is in Swindon. I was in a *youth* club.
Sylvia There you are. That's like the Junior Carlton. And later on you'll move on to the proper grown-up club in St James's.
Steve I don't know London all that well. I used to stay with my auntie in Wood Green. I don't think she was in a club.

Westminster Chimes sound the hour

Sylvia Hey, listen, that's six o'clock.
Steve The gharrie leaves at half-past. We better get dressed.
Sylvia Where are we playing tonight?
Steve R.A.F., Changi.

They begin dressing in clothes that are strewn on the bed and chairs

Sylvia Whenever I hear the Westminster Chime from St. Andrew's Cathedral I imagine I'm in England.
Steve How badly d'you want to go?
Sylvia Mummy and I talked of nothing else. Just think, she never even saw the Boat Race except on Gaumont-British news.
Steve But I mean not just visit. Do you want to stay forever?
Sylvia Of course I do.
Steve Then—the answer's easy.
Sylvia Easy?
Steve Easy as falling off a log.

Partly dressed, he now sings like Fred Astaire

> I've just had an inspiration,
> The solution's clear to me.
> Take it as an invitation
> And it's marked R.S.V.P.

Sylvia Nothing is so fine or so divine as being able to say yes
But until she's heard the question how can any lady acquiesce?
Steve Come, I want you to lead me a dance!
Why don't you give our rhythm a chance?
Our partnership could be something big,
You've already taught me to do the jig-jig,
And now that I know how lovely it feels,
Let's show the world a clean pair of heels.
Please answer, darling, don't leave me in doubt.
It's better far than sitting this life out.

The music continues, repeating the chorus while they talk and finish dressing

I told you—as easy as pie.
Sylvia D'you mean—you want me to be your partner for life?
Steve If you were a British soldier's wife, they'd have to take you home, so why don't you marry me?
Sylvia You'd honestly do that for my sake?
Steve No, for mine. Of course, we'd have to make sure the army would, in fact, pay your passage. I'll have to see Sergeant-Major Drummond.

Sylvia No! Major Flack. Your commanding officer must grant an interview on personal grounds. That's in King's Regulations.

Steve Right. I'll say: "Permission to marry Miss Morgan, sir, so that we can do the jig-jig every night, sah, and every morning and every afternoon, sah!"

Sylvia Hell's bells, you've got a lot to learn.
(*Singing*)

> Already we're an elegant pair,
> In time we'll both be floating on air.
> Here's some tuition that never fails,
> Put on your top hat, your white tie, and tails,
> And dance, as long as the orchestra plays
> Quick-stepping to the end of our days.
> We'll show the others what love's all about.
> It's better far than sitting this life out.

During the reprise of the music she teaches him new steps, using sticks and top hats from the tin trunk. At the end they go off as they sing

Both   It's better far than sitting this life—
Steve   I'm your partner—
Sylvia   I'll be your wife—
Both   Better far than sitting this life out.

Sylvia and Steve go, as Reg appears from the door of her room, watching them

The tabs close

SCENE 10

Our Sergeant-Major

Reg speaks to himself

Reg I should have known! Our Bonnie Black Madrassi's always been one to mix business and pleasure. She not only contacts their intelligence agent but lets him slip her a length into the bargain. Excuse my French but I'm under pressure. (*He suddenly shouts*) Lee! I bet they think they've got me over a barrel. Well, you watch it, Sergeant Flowers, don't go up any dark alleys. (*He shouts*) Cheng!

Lee appears from the other direction

Reg is startled to find him

Ah, Lee! Harkee. Missee Morgan shop me to police. Me no can go my flat, no can go Missee's room. Police search my billet, too, but you got my revolver, yes?

Lee nods

Cheng enters

Okay. You blingee me chop-chop.

Lee goes

Cheng, Special Investigation Blanch think they got me by short and curlee. But me ex-copper. Missee Morgan have to get her knees velly brown to catch me. (*Taking out his handkerchief to wipe his palms, he speaks again to himself*) As you were, her knees *are* brown! She's brown all over. Except for where she's black and blue. That was an error, I see that now, but I was provoked. I won't have pushy tarts on my patch. (*He becomes aware of Cheng watching and waiting*) Listen! You tell your Commie boss: if police catch me, me spillee beans. Savvy? Your boss catch plenty trouble.

Lee enters with a revolver and gives it to Reg

Good boy, Lee. You my friend. You both my friends. We together. (*He loads the gun while talking*) Your people in jungle need me keep quiet. Me know plenty, can tell plenty. But you all help me hold tongue. Number One Job: Sergeant spy go on guard tonight but maybe he not come off, okay? Softee softee catchee monkey. Number Two, we deal with Missee. (*He begins to talk to himself again*) What made you shop me, Sylvia? Just the bruises? That's only my way. I'd have taken you home to see your grannie in Swansea. I would! But now . . . (*He recovers, speaks to the Chinese*) So tell your boss I need your help and see me by-and-by.

Reg shakes hands with Lee and Cheng, smiles, and goes

Chinese percussion. Lee and Cheng look at each other. Lee quickly gestures to Cheng to follow Reg

Cheng exits after Reg, Lee the other way

Darkness. The tabs open to full stage. There are sounds of heavy rain, nocturnal animals. A long lightning flash reveals a figure in a bush-hat and monsoon cape on guard duty. This is Steve. He leans his rifle against a tree and brings out a torch to read from a letter

Steve "Dear Heather, in your last missive you remarked how much you envied me here in the lovely tropical sunshine. As I seem to remember you being top of our class in geography . . ."

A nearby whistle makes him look to the far side of stage. He waits, then returns to his letter

   "—perhaps you will recall that Singapore's climate is characterized by far heavier rainfall than you ever get in Fernleaze Crescent. Tonight, for example . . ."

The whistle is heard again. Steve moves a few paces towards it

Hello, anyone there? I mean—who goes there?

Lee comes on behind Steve and takes his rifle

Steve returns to his place and goes on with the letter

"Tonight, for example, I am on guard duty in a virtual deluge, which means standing under a tree with a rifle and fixed bayonet for two hours at a time . . ."

Reg appears and approaches Steve, holding his revolver towards him

Another whistle makes Reg hesitate and turn, as Lee runs from behind Steve, and as Reg turns back he is run through by the bayonet. He falls with a groan

Halt, who goes there? Christ, where's my gun?

Steve looks for the gun and finds it missing; he shines his torch in Lee's face

Friend or foe?

Cheng comes on the other side and calls to Lee. They go off into the jungle

Halt or I—blow my whistle! (*He moves after them but falls over Reg's body*) Who's that? Reg! What's up?
Reg Bastard!
Steve You hurt? (*He touches him, finds the wound and looks at his bloody hand*) Christ! . . . Get you what? . . . Who won't get you? Don't talk any more, I'll call for help. (*He goes to the side and shouts*) Love! Sergeant Love! Anyone, come here, quick! (*He blows a piercing whistle, then returns to Reg, who is still muttering*) What you doing creeping about in the dark? Who knifed you? . . . The S.I.B.? . . . What's the S.I.B. got to do with it?

Eric comes on, naked but for boots, but with a gun

Eric What's the palaver? Swindon, is that you?
Steve Love, over here! What you doing bollock-naked?
Eric I've been standing in the monsoon rain trying to cure my prickly heat.
Steve Look, the Sergeant-Major's hurt. Help me carry him to the guard-room.
Eric What? Hullo, Chiefy—he's talking—what's he saying? . . . What's the S.I.B.?
Steve Take his feet.
Eric He's bleeding. Lord, he's covered in blood.
Steve Stop nattering, for Christ's sake!
Eric I can hardly see with all this rain on my glasses. All right, Chiefy, *nil desperandum* . . . you'll be all right.

Eric and Steve carry Reg off into the darkness

SCENE 11

Lest We Forget

The rain stops. The Lights come up brightly on a bare stage. A march beat is heard on the drum. Len marches on, K.D., carrying a clipboard, and wearing a black armband

Len Right, guard of honour, form up, stand easy, but pay attention. Major Flack has detailed me as senior N.C.O. to be i/c the cortège. I only want to say one thing before we fetch the body from the mortuary. Remember, this is a military funeral and will be tantamount to a church parade. So best behaviour, mind. No acting like cunts in the House of the Lord. Squad, attention, right turn, quick march, hef, right, hef, right . . .

Lee and Cheng come on with shovels and prepare a grave-trap. Terri comes on as Len goes off. He wears Officer's K.D. with arm-band

Terri We were all ordered on that parade. I thought of wearing the little black number from our Latin-American Medley but no, it had to be the full captain's drag with only a discreet arm-band. I chose the fairly butch day-slap, no rouge or lipstick and the merest suspicion of eye-shadow. Well, funerals and weddings play havoc with mascara.

The drum starts again, now muffled, as Charles, Kevin, Steve and Eric enter bearing a coffin draped with the Union Jack, slow-marching. Len enters with a rifle

And as soon as the Tiller Girls carried her in, there wasn't a dry eye in the cemetery.

Giles follows: K.D., with his sword at the present. The bearers turn up-stage and place the coffin over the trap. Sylvia is last, also in black

All arrive at the trap as the bearers lower the coffin on ropes

When the padre said "In the midst of life we are in death", I thought well, many a true word spoken in jest.

Giles In sure and certain hope of the resurrection to eternal life, through our Lord Jesus Christ . . .

Len fires a round into the air. Terri puts his hands on his ears

Terri They always do that, apparently, when some queen's given her all on active service. I said, well, I've done that many a time and never got more than a port-and-lemon.

Terri joins the funeral group. The mourners throw earth on the coffin. The muffled drum resumes and the bearers march away, forming behind Giles as he moves down to address the audience. The Chinese shovel earth into the trap. As Giles speaks, the Lights fade and the cloth comes down

Giles We mourn the loss of our comrade-in-arms. Both as a man and a Company Sergeant-Major, Mr Drummond deserved the admiration of us all. Not least in his attention to detail. Nothing was too trivial, be it in the insubordination of a native bearer, the detection of women's perfume in the men's ablutions, or the prevention of rabies. He was not, by his own admission, a God-fearing man. Indeed, fear was not in his

nature. But in his care for you young men, his concern that none of you be corrupted by waste or idleness, he retained many qualities from his previous service as a London bobby: dependability, discipline, devotion to duty. This devotion it was that led to his savage murder, for it was he who went out in heavy rain to inspect the guard and came instead upon the gang of Communistic Chinamen who disembowelled him. (*He pauses, clears his throat, moves and resumes*) It should not have needed this atrocity to awaken us to our danger but it has. Like the British here in Forty-One, Forty-Two; drowsily playing cricket on a lawn beside a Gothic Cathedral. And if you'd said, "But look here, you should be arming yourselves, the yellow men are on the way," they'd have answered, "My dear chap, Britannia rules the waves, remember. If their tinpot ships try to sail into Singapore, our great guns will pick them off like pigeons." Well, as you know, our friends from Tokyo came the other way. Down through the mainland riding bikes. Across the causeway, ting-a-ling, "velly solly, no more clicket now." It's not funny, sergeant! Let us give thanks to God for this ghastly warning. Heaven be praised we've heard the bicycle bells in time. And look here, it makes no odds that this is a song-and-dance unit. Never send to know for whom the bells toll. They toll for *thee*. Me. All of us.
(*He sings*)

> Behold the army of the Prince of Peace
> Conquering that his kingdom may increase
> Taking to some distant Asian shore
> His cleansing and redemption evermore.

All Many a laughing savage lives and dies
> In ignorance of Jesus' sacrifice
> And sun-kissed children swing beneath the palms
> Hid from the mercy-mercy-mercy of his loving arms.
> > Amen.

They go off

SCENE 12
Tea for Three

The cloth goes up on Sylvia's room. She's sitting on her bed, still in black. In the wicker armchair is Lee, in white shirt and trousers. There is a tray of tea-things on the tin-trunk and they are both drinking from cups.

Steve opens the door and enters, wearing K.D., and sees Lee

Sylvia Hullo, darling.

Steve leaves the door open, comes forward, takes off his beret and stares at Lee

The Major kept you a long time. What did he have to say?

No answer, Steve stares at Lee who stands and finishes his tea

Are you going, Mr Lim?

Lee puts his cup on the tray, bows to her, then him and goes to the door. She follows

You won't need to come again.

Lee shakes his head, smiles and goes

She shuts the door. Steve throws his beret down and moves away. Sylvia moves towards him

Terri dropped me here right after the funeral. I thought you'd be coming straight away. I kept on my dress so that you could take it off.

He continues round the room, away from her. She follows some way, then goes to pour tea

I'm also wearing the black underwear we bought in the shop in Stamford Road, d'you remember? (*She approaches him with a cup of tea*) Darling . . .

He takes the tea, sips it, looks at it and makes a sour face

Steve What's this? Where's the milk and sugar?

Sylvia You don't have milk or sugar with China tea.

Steve China?

Sylvia Lapsang Suchong. Fortnum's sell it in Middle Road.

Steve You sit here with a bloody Chinaman drinking China tea, still wearing the dress you wore to Reg's funeral! Why didn't you get the bloody *China*man to take it off?

Sylvia Steve, you're not jealous?

Steve Jealous? God Almighty, what's jealousy got to do with it? I'm talking about being British. All right? Because, whatever you say, you're not—not by a long chalk. But I am British. And Major Flack's been talking to us and he made me see we're on one side and the Chinks are on the other. And then I find you actually being touched up by that slant-eyed fuck-pig. (*He takes up the tray and throws it across the floor with a clatter of tin and broken crockery. For some moments he stands*)

Sylvia Mr Lim came here to see Reg. Reg used this place to meet his clients and associates and I was required to entertain them. Mr Lim was a middle man. A contact with the garment trade, I think. Getting the costumes made for SADUSEA that hardly ever appear on the stage. They were paid for and signed for by the army but most of them were used in Reg's sideline . . .

Steve Sideline?

Sylvia Boy prostitutes.

Steve Well, if Reg hadn't done it, someone else would.

Sylvia Absolutely.

Steve That bloody Chinaman, I suppose . . .

Sylvia Mister Lim didn't enjoy his work.

Steve Why did he do it then?

Sylvia Reg had some kind of hold over him. Gambling debts, I don't know.

Steve What hold did he have over you?

Sylvia You've seen these bruises? That was for answering back at the dress-rehearsal.

Steve (*after a pause*) Did he have any other sidelines?

Sylvia Import-export. Thai silk, jade, works of art looted from Buddhist temples, opium and gun-running.

Steve Gun-running? Come on . . .

Sylvia Only to protect his own interests at first, but then he realized there was a very steady demand from the Communists. So he formed a partnership.

Steve You're taking the piss. (*He holds her threateningly by the wrist*) D'you think I'm a moon man? Think I've just come out?

She bites his hand. He lets go. He sucks his hand

Christ!

Sylvia He formed a partnership with a captain in the ordnance corps! They supply the Communists from the armoury in the transit camp.

Steve (*moving after her*) Proof! You better give me proof or Christ, I'll . . .

Sylvia What? What? Take me to the interrogation room? Why d'you think that had to be white-washed so often? Because of the blood-stained walls!

Steve That only shows he was a bully. Give me proof he was selling guns to the Commics.

Sylvia I can't. D'you think he *told me* anything? I used to be sent out whenever they got down to business but I do remember one night, I was out there, Reg was very angry with a Chinese man in here. He was shouting something about the C.O.'s staff car. They must have used it to make deliveries of arms out of the camp and on to the mainland—then one night on the way back the driver had gone into a tree or something...

Steve And the car had been burnt out on the Bukit Timah Road.

Sylvia You knew all the time.

Steve It was after that Major Flack made him draw up a guard roster.

Sylvia That's right.

Steve And one night he goes to inspect that guard . . .

Sylvia Oh, no. He went to kill you.

Steve Me?

Sylvia He knew he was about to be arrested and he'd always believed you were a spy sent to catch him.

Steve And instead he got killed himself? Who by?

Sylvia The Communists. To keep his mouth shut for good about terrorist hide-outs on the mainland.

Steve Who told you all this?

Sylvia Mister Lim. They're as thick as thieves, these Chinese.

He comes to her, embraces her, kisses her and looks at her dress

Steve Is this one of those costumes? Take it off.

Sylvia turns her back and he opens the dress

And don't ever wear it again. Or anything else he gave you.
Sylvia All right. Now come to bed . . .

The Lights in the room fade as Sylvia goes to the gramophone, puts on the record of "Greensleeves", and gets into bed. Steve comes down and speaks to the audience

Steve Dear Everyone at Fifty-Six, I'm sorry to hear from Dad that the spirit of post-war idealism hasn't lasted. I still believe education is the only hope for the world, though of course in the light of experience it won't be nearly as easy as I once imagined. In fact, life seems more complicated every day. If one genius may paraphrase another, there are more things in heaven and earth than are dreamt of in Fernleaze Crescent. Tell Heather I'll be writing as soon as I . . .
Sylvia Steve! Come on!
Steve Must dash now. In haste. Love to everyone. Steve.

Steve goes up to the bed as the music swells, and—

the CURTAIN *falls*

ACT II

Scene 1

Noël, Noël

Terri comes before the tabs wearing a dinner-jacket, carrying a cigarette-holder, and sings:

Terri   Dear whomever it may concern at the B.B.C.,
Pass this letter to the Brains Trust very urgently.

> Throughout the war we have soldiered on
> When almost every hope had gone
> And pinned our flagging faith to Vera Lynn.
> We turned our railings into tanks
> And smiled politely at the Yanks
> When all they sent across was Errol Flynn.

But when the lights went on we saw the vict'ry was a sham,
The lion's share turned out to be a smaller slice of spam.

> The bluebirds came onc dreary day,
> Looked at Dover and flew away
> And grim spectators murmured "Why can't I?"
> They might go down to the sea in ships
> But that's forbidden by Stafford Cripps

And the nightingale in Berkeley Square can only sit and cry:

Could you please inform us who it was that won the war?
The outcome isn't certain, Heaven knows.
Now everyone's so keen to put the Germans on their feet,
For apparently
The majority
Are really rather sweet.
Meanwhile back in Britain we're still lining up in rows
To buy enough to keep ourselves alive.
So could you please inform us how we came to lose the war
That we won in nineteen forty-five?

> Land of Clement Atlee
> Where the teeth are free!
> Our former wealth is going to
> Augment the Inland Revenue
> And though our situation might seem hard
> At least you needn't work these days,
> The Ministry of Labour pays
> You well, provided someone's stamped your card.

The National Health is failing fast and no-one gives a fig,
The corpse will look delightful in a newly-issued wig.
> Our image for posterity
> Is one of grim austerity,
> The socialist Nirvana's on the way:
> New ministries proliferate
> Whose function is to allocate
To everyone his fair and proper share of sweet F.A.

> Room five hundred and four
> Has met a somewhat grisly fate;
> Now everything's in duplicate
> That fourteenth Heaven on the old tenth floor
> Is room one thousand and eight

So—could you please inform us how we came to lose the peace?
Perhaps it's best to be the losing side,
Now that the Americans are sponsoring the Japs,
Taking the view
That but for a few
They're awfully decent chaps.
Such a strange development is wounding to our pride
The countrymen of Wellington and Clive.
So Berlin only knows how Britain came to lose the peace,
When she won in nineteen forty-five
Four, three, two, one,
Yes *won* in nineteen forty-five?

Terri goes. The tabs rise or part

SCENE 2

Kernel of the Knuts

The backcloth is an office wall, featuring a large map of Malaya and a photo of George VI. There are two chairs, and a plain desk. Cheng is at the desk, pouring tea into a cup. Giles enters and addresses the audience

Giles Why did we lose the peace? I can answer that question. There was never a peace to lose. There was only a temporary truce and a slight change of enemy. No sooner had the Yanks exploded that contraption than bands of agitators turned from killing Japs to killing us. Well, now at last it's official—"an emergency" they're calling it, but everyone knows it's the start of the Third World War. Soon as . . .

Lee comes on with Steve, who salutes

Steve Sergeant Flowers, sir.
Giles Ah, yes. Stand easy. I'd offer you tea but it's China.

Steve I like China tea, sir.
Giles Ming! Another cup.

Cheng goes

Sit down.

Steve sits

I understand the tour of Singapore Island is being well-received.
Steve They seem to like it, yessir.
Giles No accounting for taste. But then I'm no judge. Last time I saw a show was—what?—nineteen thirty-five. Puerile drivel. Once saw half a film and walked out. Can't conceive why anyone wastes their time with it when they might be reading Bunyan or the Bard.

Cheng returns with a cup and pours for both

Or learning to tell one constellation from another. One bird from another. Most of them don't know a wren from a tit.

Lee and Cheng stand together by the door

Steve Sir.

Giles sits and looks at the papers on the desk

Giles Thank you, Ming. Glowing reports on you as company manager. Miss Morgan, for instance, says you grow more capable every day. Captain Dennis particularly praises the way you've handled the business end. Even Sergeant Bonny, as far as I can make out from his semiliterate scrawl, confirms your qualities of leadership. Now. As you know, there's a war on.
Steve You mean the state of emergency?
Giles That's softy-softly officialese. The Communists used to call themselves the Malayan People's Anti-Japanese Army; now it's the Anti-British Army. What's that if not a declaration of war? I immediately applied for posting to an active command. I want to serve my God, my king and my country. Are you a Christian?
Steve I was in the choir for a time, sir.
Giles Churchgoing family?
Steve My father manages the local Co-op. He believes more in fair shares, moderation.
Giles What do you believe in?
Steve Well, Education, first, sir, then . . .
Giles Not good enough. Why don't you sign on with Christ? Oh, I know what you're going to say, you're going to say, "Yes, but look here, I didn't ask him to go and die for me on the cross like that."
Steve Well, sir, I didn't. I wasn't even born.
Giles Be your age, Sergeant, look beyond your nose. You'd better start believing in something. We'd *all* better. Because *they* do. The Russians, the Chinese, the Malayan People's Anti-British Army. *What*, d'you think?

Steve Sir?

Giles *What* do they believe in?

Steve Equality, sir? Fair shares? Social justice?

Giles Exactly. Pie in the sky. Jam tomorrow. Take equality. Think of Sergeant Bonny. Look at Bonny's handwriting. Visualize Bonny's brain. Out of the sewers of Birmingham into the jungles of Malaya. Backbone of the army, of course, loyal to a fault, obedient, dependable. But is Stalin going to give him command of a division out of a belief in equality? Is he? Yes or no?

Steve Well, sir, what Marx actually said was from each according to his ability . . .

Giles No's the answer. Because Uncle Joe is a wily old bounder and Bonny's as dim as a nun's night-light. He might just let him command a latrine. And indeed so would I. No more. So much for equality, a notion by which millions of child-like people are led into prison-camps. Millions of Bonnys. And make no mistake, they must be led one way or another. Either into Siberia or the Kingdom of Heaven.

Steve I think, sir, that if education begins early enough . . .

Giles You can't educate what isn't there. The Bonnys of this world must be *told*. They *want* to be. Form fours. Present arms. Stand easy. And someone has to tell them. Me, of course. Or Mister Drummond. Or, since his murder, perhaps—you.

Steve Me, sir?

Giles Our unit's strength is short of one sergeant-major. I can apply for a new sergeant-major or I can make you up to that rank. How d'you feel about sharing the burden of command?

Steve Sorry, sir. Are you . . .

Giles I'm offering you a crown. D'you want time to think it over?

Steve No, sir. I'd like to help you—like to share the burden, sir.

They shake hands

Giles Well done, well done! I shan't pretend this isn't going to be a tough assignment. We may well get into a spot of bother up-country.

Steve You mean because of H.Q. saying we've got to charge admission?

Giles What?

Steve The shows have always been free before, sir, the men may not take to it kindly. I know it's only a few cents but . . .

Giles I said *trouble*, son. Bandits—Communistic Terrorists . . .

Steve But since the Emergency started . . .

Giles Since the war broke out . . .

Steve Yessir, isn't our tour confined to the coastal area? (*He points to the map*) Kuala Lumpur, Ipoh, Penang, Butterworth, not many bandits there, sir.

Giles Look here, Sergeant, it may have been someone's idea of a joke to give me command of a concert-party but command it I do and our itinerary is no business of the desk-wallahs at G.H.Q. I'm reverting to the one worked out by Sarnt-Major Drummond.

Steve Sarnt-Major . . . ?

Cheng goes to the desk to collect the tea, and wipes the desk. Giles lifts his papers to facilitate him, Cheng reads the papers as he does so

Giles Precisely. Good thinking. What you and the S.I.B. have told me since his death makes it clear he was using the concert-party as a decoy for illegal arms-trafficking. Well, what if the show's *still* a decoy?

Steve You mean set a trap?

Giles Precisely. With the artistes as bait.

Steve But we're not an armed unit, sir.

Giles We will be—armed and ready. How's that for a Jungle Jamboree, eh? Somewhere here—(*pointing to the map*)—after the Cameron Highlands. That's where we'll flush them out of cover. So we'll play to everyone—not only British but Malays, Gurkhas, Indians . . .

Steve Will they understand the show, d'you think?

Cheng turns to look at the map then collects the tea

Giles Give them a splash of colour, plenty of movement. You've got a conjurer, haven't you?

Cheng goes off with the tea

Giles locks the paper in a drawer

Steve Yessir.

Giles Dancing girls?

Steve One, sir. Miss Morgan. Matter of fact, that's why I applied for this personal interview. To ask your permission to marry her.

Giles The Anglo girl?

Steve Yes.

Giles Handsome.

Steve I think so, sir.

Giles Women of mixed blood often are. Early on. Snag is, they tend to put on weight rather soon. How old is she?

Steve Twenty-eight.

Giles (*whistling amazement*) That almost certainly means thirty. When you're thirty she'll be forty. Middle-aged. And, of course, they find it difficult settling down in the U.K. Climate's not what they're used to. They don't like the food.

Steve Oh, she's very British, sir. Her dad was in the Welsh Fusiliers.

Giles Welsh and Indian? Combustible mixture. Don't say anything to her till you're perfectly sure in your own mind.

Steve I've already asked her, sir. And been accepted.

Giles (*sighing*) She's after a free trip home, you see. Quite a consideration. On the other hand, they don't take an engagement as seriously as English girls. Remember you're going to have your work cut out up-country. You'll need *mens sana in corpore sano*. If you understand me?

Steve (*after a pause*) A sound mind in a healthy body.

Giles Yes, but do you catch my drift?

Steve I'm not sure, sir.

Giles Difficult. I have no son. Daughters, yes, but my wife handled all
that, of course. How's your French?

Steve All right, up to School Certificate.

Giles *Alors—vous savez—physiquement les femmes orientales sont très
belles, très mignons, n'est-ce-pas?*

Steve *Biensûr, mon commandant.*

Giles *Mais il y a toujours la possibilité d'attraper les maladies . . .*

Steve *Maladies?*

Giles *Les maladies d'amour.*

Steve Illnesses of love? Ah, *oui*, love-sickness.

Giles No, that's *mal d'amour*. I was using *amour* in its other sense, of
Eros or Venus.

Steve The illnesses of—I'm sorry, sir . . .

Giles Look, all I mean to say is: mull it over while we're out on tour. See
a bit less of her for a few weeks. Meanwhile I'll get the wheels in motion
for your crown. Wong!

Lee comes forward and opens the door for Steve

I needn't tell you this is all top secret. Strictly between the two of us.

Steve *Entre nous*, sir.

Giles Good thinking.

Steve Sir! And thank you.

Giles Thank you, Sergeant. Command can be lonely.

Steve goes

Lee remains, hands Giles his cap and he comes downstage

Lee and Cheng go

Dear Margaret, there's a young soldier here I'd like to invite down to the
mill-house when I get home. Decent, intelligent boy, very much the kind
I'd have liked as a son, had God so willed. He's in a spot of bother at the
moment but I mean to help him out of that. As I would my own. (*Moving
off, putting on his cap*) How splendid your roses winning first prize again
this year . . .

Giles goes

SCENE 3

A Tricycle Made for Three

*The office cloth is flown; the furniture is removed by Cheng in black. On to
a clear stage with night lighting Lee drives a trishaw in which Terri and
Sylvia are sitting. He pulls up and waits. They get out. The piano plays a
ballad accompaniment to this scene*

Sylvia Terri!

Terri Good night, lovie.

Sylvia Thank you. Thank you so much! (*She kisses him and hugs him*)

Terri My dear, what have I done? Given you a lift home in a trishaw? You mustn't sell your favours so cheap.

Sylvia Oh, good heavens, it isn't that! I'm thanking you for bringing Steve and me together and for making me so happy.

Terri Oh, there again I was only being the good fairy. I rather fancied her first of all but baby-snatching's not my line and she had so much to learn . . .

Sylvia Oh, didn't he? Even now I keep on finding how little he knows. When I told him I was going to have his baby, for instance, he asked me how I could tell. D'you know, he thought babies came out of the woman's stomach? Out of her navel!

Terri Feminine hygiene's still no part of an English education.

Sylvia Imagine, at twenty years of age not knowing that.

Terri But anyway she understands now?

Sylvia I think so, yes. I did some drawings.

Terri And everything's all right?

Sylvia He's going to see the major soon. And, listen, d'you think it's a good idea, I suggested Steve should ask him to be best man?

Terri Major Flack? Why not indeed?

Sylvia And how would you feel about giving the bride away? I've no living relatives here.

Terri If I must, but I shan't enjoy it.

Sylvia Why ever not?

Terri I've only just found you, a partner in a million. And next we know you'll be standing there with a swollen belly saying "I will" to a hushed congregation.

Sylvia Will you do it or no?

Terri I certainly won't let anyone else.

Sylvia Thank you again. (*She kisses him*) For everything.

Terri Good night, duckie.

Sylvia goes

Now what shall I wear? The white suit from the Jolson Medley would be discreet. Or perhaps the dark dress with the half-veil. Tremendously dignified, with everyone whispering "Who *is* she?" and "It's Greer Garson!"

Lee, waiting with the trishaw, rings the bell. Terri turns to him

Thank you, Ada. (*He climbs aboard*)
        Your Fairy Queen's done all the good she may
        So Fleet Club, sweetie, by the shortest way!

Lee rings the bell and drives off, Terri waves and blows kisses to us

SCENE 4

Privates on Parade

Steve marches on with S-M insignia, leading the squad all in K.D.: Len, Kevin, Charles and Eric. The drum beats as they march

Steve By the front—quick march! Eff, right, eff, right, eff, right. Squad—halt! Left—turn! Order—hype!

Giles enters

Giles Stand the men easy, Sarnt-Major.

Steve Squad, stand at—ease! Stand easy.

Giles The tour of Singapore is now over and the time has come for us to go up-country. Bring a bit of song-and-dance to those chaps who suddenly find themselves chasing bandits in the ulu. Ulu. That's the jungle. But one or two of you might be saying, "Yes, that's all very well but half a mo, here's the old man telling us to go up-country, likely to get in a spot of bother with the bandits, while he's here in a cushy billet. Seems a rum kind of a go." And you'd be right. But I'm not staying here. I'm coming *with* you. I dare say one or two of you are thinking, "Just a tick, what use is he gonna be in a show? Reckon by the looks of him he's got a tin ear and two left feet." And that again would be good thinking. You must be able to look after yourselves if there's any trouble. And that's where I can help. During the next few days I'll be putting you through a refresher course in basic training: small arms drill, grenade throwing, unarmed combat plus as much of a notion of conditions in the ulu as I can give you before the off. So carry on, Sarnt-Major.

Steve Sir. Right. Get fell in. Squad! Squad—'shun! Right—dress. From the right number!

Line-up One—two—three—four.

Steve Slope—hype! By the right, quick—march! Eff, right, eff, right, eff, right. About turn! About turn! About turn! Eff, right, eff, right, eff, right. Squad—halt! Left turn!

Giles salutes and everyone sings a rousing march, with martial choreography

All   Come, see the Privates on Parade
You'll say "How proudly they're displayed."
And when we hear the music of a milit'ry band
You'll be amazed how smartly we can take our stand.

For when the bugles sound attack
Up goes the good old Union Jack.
You may as well surrender when you hear our battle-cry
There'll be no more escaping when we raise our weapons high

> And in the vict'ry cavalcade
> You'll see the Privates on Parade.

After much countermarching to music, they exit, leaving Giles, who detains Len

Giles Sarnt Bonny, a word with you. As you know, you're in line for another stripe. I've been watching you on the square. Well done. But leadership also calls for qualities of tact, diplomacy, understanding.

Len I ain't never gone after promotion . . .

Giles So let's suppose we're faced with a tricky situation here and now, shall we? See how we'd cope. Here's a platoon of squaddies lined up and you've got to announce some tragic news to just one man. Here he is in Singapore and home in England his mother has suddenly, unexpectedly died. How d'you break it to him?

Len (*after a pause*) What's his name, sir?

Giles (*impatiently*) Not important. Charlie Farnes-Barnes. Come on, Bonny, thinking on your feet, another of the qualities of leadership.

Len Squad—shun! Private Farnes-Barnes, one step forward march. Right, son, pay attention, your mother's dead.

Giles Hell's bells, man, you'll have him in sick bay suffering from shock. Think of something more subtle, a roundabout approach. Indirect.

Len (*after thinking*) Right, squad, shun! Pay attention. All those men going to see their mothers next time they're on leave, one pace forward march—where the fuck are you going, Farnes-Barnes?

The men enter, marching, with Terri and Sylvia

Steve Ready, aim, fire! BANG!
All   We are the C. of E. Brigade.
Steve Fire! BANG!
All   We're marching on a new crusade
Steve Fire! BANG!

There are no lyrics to the next couplet, but dialogue over marching

Terri (*to Steve*) Vada the little tiaras, duckie.
Steve What?
Terri The crowns on your sleeve.
Steve Oh.
Terri Bona. Suits you.
All   You'll need a piece of four-by-two
          To get a really good pull-through.
          The enemy's resisting and the trumpet sounds advance
          They'd best lay down their arms because they haven't got a chance
          Faced with the cocksure cannonade
          Of the Privates on Parade.

Steve puts them through paces as Sergeant-Major

Then they exit

Giles retains Kevin this time

Giles Cartwright!

Kevin Sir.

Giles More to your liking, Cartwright?

Kevin What, sir?

Giles More like being a soldier?

Kevin Oh. Do with a bit more jungle training, not so much bull.

Giles All in good time.

Kevin We don't hold with bull in the R.A.F.

Giles You were air crew, weren't you?

Kevin Navigator bomb-aimer. I joined under-age to get a crack at Jerry. Soon as I passed out flight-sergeant, ready to go on ops, old Adolf packs it in. Right, I thought to myself, see if we can't chalk up a few Nips. No sooner reach Ceylon than Tojo says *he* don't want to play no more. (*He shakes his head sympathetically*) I put in for my release. I said, "You want a navigator bomb-aimer to drive a lorry for three years?" Jesus Christ Almighty! A few weeks sooner I could have bombed Dresden.

The others come on as Giles sings

Giles A word to the wise, Flight-Sergeant.
      (*He sings*)
      Wise soldiers generally refrain
      From taking Jesus' name in vain.
      One day you'll need to call him in the clamour of a war
      Then he would say "Look here, you've often called on me before.
      I'm an extremely busy bloke.
      You shouldn't use my name in joke."

All   And when we're standing on parade
      Each with his rifle and grenade
      You'll hear the sergeant cry:

Steve   Presenting arms to the right!

All   And all the girls declare "they've never seen such a sight".
      To know that God is on our side
      Makes every private swell with pride.
      We'll press upon our enemy until he's in a funk

Giles   And show him it's no easy thing
      Resisting British spunk.

All   He'll feel the forceful fusillade
      Of the Privates on Parade.

Giles watches as they practise unarmed combat. At the end he gives orders

Giles Right, well done, fall out, gather round.

They obey, crouching downstage facing up, while Giles briefs

The Malayan peninsula is slightly smaller than England and Wales and four-fifths impenetrable jungle. Rich in game but also crawling with every kind of hazard—soldier ants, centipedes, scorpions, typhus tics, leeches—and if *they* don't worry you the plants tear your clothes and the grass cuts like a saw. By day it's deathly quiet but at nightfall pandemonium breaks out as all these chaps get weaving on their various chores. Yet the odds are all you'll see will be a few fireflies or the eyes of a panther. Which might or might not be the signals of a Chinese terrorist.

Terri Major, I'm sure my contract stipulates we'll be doing the Number One Tour and keeping to the main roads. There's nothing about the jungle.

Giles No need for alarm, Mr Dennis. We'll be following the route taken by the previous parties, the route planned by Mr Drummond. But: this country is a powder keg. Even the main roads are a death trap. Once we're on the mainland, we'll be in the front line. A theatre of war.

All   You may as well surrender when you hear our battle cry.
There'll be no more escaping when we raise our weapons high.
And in the vict'ry cavalcade
You'll see the Privates on Parade.

We're Sadusea
And on the other hand we're glad to see
You've come along tonight to . . .

We've taken pains
To see our show's the sort that entertains

What can we do for the rest of the chorus?
They know who we are, so they know . . .

Entertains
To see our show's the sort that entertains
To see our show's the sort that entertains
Entertains
Entertains
S.A.D.U.S.E.A.
Song and Dance Unit, South East A . . . sia.

They march off

The Lights change

SCENE 5

The Midnight Choo-Choo

Sounds of a steam train are heard and clouds of vapour are blown about in flashing lights. Music represents a labouring engine, and a whistle suggests a departing train. All but Reg, Cheng and Lee enter in a row, working arms together like pistons. Gradually they accelerate, singing whistle sounds together and working their way across the stage. They haul a truck representing a railway compartment: a bench each side, a table between, windows and a corridor upstage. Lee and Cheng come on with large cards naming places on

*the journey: Johore Bahru and Kluang. Others continue with Tampin, Kotan,
etc. Perhaps the Malayan map has dropped in behind and their journey is
traced by a moving spot. Len, Kevin, Charles and Eric occupy the benches,
smoking, playing cards, etc. Lee stands in the corridor wearing railway cap,
as a ticket inspector*

Len Kiswasti you come, Johnny? You want dekko railway warrants? You
go ekdum sergeant-major sahib juldi juldi. Doosrah compartment.
Burra sahib keep warrants sub-cheese fucking sahibs and mem-sahib.
You get pukka shufti, malam? Tikh-hai.

Lee nods and goes

The sound of the travelling train continues

Charles He was Malayan.
Len I know that.
Charles They don't speak Hindustani.
Kevin *That* what it was?
Len Fucking understood anyroad.
Kevin You can't even speak the King's English.
Len I can speak the King's fucking English better than any Cockney
fucker, now then!
Kevin Not without effing and blinding every other word.
Charles Right. Time for another five minutes with the swear-box. (*He puts
a small tin money-box on the table*) You've got your small change out for
cards. And remember I'm the referee, if I say it's swearing it is.
Len Already had this once today. I'm nearly fucking skint.
Charles One.
Len Oh, fuck it.
Charles Two.

Len puts two coins in the box

Len Deal the cards so we don't have to talk.

*Kevin collects the pack. Eric performs a strange movement: he shoots out
one arm, displays a wristwatch, reaches into his pocket and brings out a
cigarette case and a lighter. He takes out an imaginary cigarette and lights
it. The others watch*

Charles What's that meant to be?
Eric What d'you *think*?
Charles Some curious tropical variant of St Vitus' Dance?
Eric I'm working out a movement for when I'm back in Blighty, to display
my Swiss watch, silver cigarette case and Ronson lighter all in one. I
haven't yet included my Parker pen but all in good time . . .
Charles I'd advise against adding any other movement. It already looks
like an epileptic seizure.
Eric Practice makes perfect, squire. And when you imagine me in rimless
specs and a Harris Tweed jacket . . .

Charles I've seen the jacket. I've seen you trying it on in the basha.

Kevin We've all seen you. Sitting there in your Chinese Harris Tweed jacket drinking lemonade.

Charles That's what aggravates your prickly heat.

Eric I happen to think a little discomfort is easily borne for the sake of cutting a dash.

Len You look like something the cat's dragged in.

They laugh

Eric Laugh away. The day I walk up Susan's garden path we'll see who's laughing . . .

Kevin How much this lighter cost you?

Eric Ten chips. Which you'll agree is rock-bottom for a genuine English Ronson.

Kevin (*looking at it carefully*) You read what it says on this genuine English Ronson? "Made in British." (*He laughs*)

Charles Oh, no. Love, you've done it again. It's Hong Kong imitation.

Eric (*looking at the lighter*) Ruddy cheek! Well, anyway, they won't know the difference back home. I'll give it to Susan's Dad. Token of my esteem.

Len Here, look at that. All that fucking panic getting off I forgot this letter come for you this morning. That's your fiancée's handwriting, ain't it? (*He gives Eric a letter*)

Charles Swearword.

Len feeds a coin into the box

Eric A New Malden postmark but it's not Susan's writing, no. Not her dad's either. (*During the following he opens and reads the letter*)

Len What about dealing them sodding cards, Lambeth?

Charles rattles the box

Sodding? (*He pays*)

This procedure continues throughout the scene

Kevin (*shuffling*) Eh, Brum, how d'you get in this skive in the first place?

Len What? Entertainments? Ain't I never told you?

Kevin Elocution, wasn't it? Shakespeare? Or was it to clean out the crapper? I forget.

Len I come in as an accordionist. Piano-fucking-accordionist. I used to be with Al Fresco and his Piano-accordion Hooligans.

Kevin Get away.

Len Straight up.

Kevin You ain't really played with them, have you?

Len (*taking out his wallet*) Ain't I never showed you the picture?

Kevin Picture?

Len Photograph. (*He shows it to Kevin*) There you are. Didn't believe me, did you?

Kevin This is just you on your own in the back yard playing the accordion.

Len What d'you think it was going to be?

Kevin I thought it was going to be with Fresco's Accordion Hooligans.

Eric stares at his letter in disbelief

Len I had to fucking practice, didn't I?

Kevin You aren't half a dopey sod. (*He pays a coin*) How d'you stand him, Charlotte?

Charles I love him—so it's easy . . . (*He becomes aware of Eric staring at the letter*) What's the matter, is Susan all right? Who's the letter from?

Eric My mucker Roy Lawrence.

Charles I remember. Billed himself as the Airman with the Flying Feet.

Eric I asked him to deliver the silk and lace for Susan's wedding dress.

Charles Oh, yes. Did he manage it?

Eric (*nodding*) She's going to marry *him* instead. "Neither of us meant this to happen but we couldn't help ourselves. It is hard to put into words but when you come home I will explain everything." (*He puts down the letter*)

The others are silent

I'll say he'll ruddy well explain everything. At the double, before he gets a bunch of fives where it hurts him most.

Charles Now, come on, Eric, take it easy . . .

Eric I'll soon have this lot sorted out, never fear. Who do they think they are, what? Damned cheek! Couldn't help themselves? Why not, would you mind telling me?

He looks at the others as though expecting an answer. Train sounds continue

Kevin Looks to me as though he's helped himself to quite a tidy slice.

Eric takes off his glasses and polishes them with his handkerchief

Eric Here have I been keeping myself for her and all of a sudden, out of the blue, I get a messpot. And she doesn't even send it, she gets *him* to send it. She and I used to do our prep together—we were tennis partners —she assisted with the magic—and now she can turn me down for . . . He never even went to a decent grammar school, just some wretched elementary . . . (*He drops his glasses and kneels to find them*)

Len goes to Eric, finds his glasses, and hands them to him

Charles Shall I make you some lemonade? You brought a tin of crystals?

Len gives Charles a tin of crystals. Eric sits in his own compartment with the letter. There is silence for a moment, except for the train wheels

Len Women? A load of cunts. (*He puts coins in the tin*)

Charles puts his hand on Len's, raises it to his lips and kisses it. Train music

   Giles enters

The tabs close behind him

Giles From Kuala Lumpur we went by road—a couple of jeeps, a fifteen hundredweight and a three-ton gharry. At the rear armed sentries, tail-boards down for a quick getaway in case of ambush. Bren guns loaded with actions cocked, mounted on the driver's cabin, raking the road ahead. Next stop, the Cameron Highlands. And then, the ulu! I felt a familiar but almost forgotten tightening of the stomach. Years of bore-dom fell away like an old skin. Now that our lives were in danger, they suddenly became infinitely precious. I prayed for our safety and thanked Almighty God that at last the real show was beginning.

Giles goes

SCENE 6

The Tabs open on Terri as Miranda, singing, with Eric and Len, in frilly shirts, accompanying him on suitable rhythmic instruments

Terri   Have you ever been
Down in Argentina
Have you ever known zat special thrill?
How d'you like to mail a
Card from Venezuela
You could find romance in Old Brazil
Think how you could brag you are
Week-ending in Nicaragua
Or wearing funny hats in Uruguay
Come and have a gala
Down in Guatemala
The Latin-American way.

As the song proceeds, they come downstage and the tabs close behind them

Every Spanish woman
Vote for Mr Truman
And she pray her favourite saint to bless
We like Coca Cola
We like Yankee dollar
We all love American Express
Come along to Haiti
Where the army's mighty
Keeping trouble-makers far away
How could you resista
Week-end with Batista
The Latin-American way.

SCENE 7

The North of Gongapooch

*Hangings or screens represent an improvised dressing-room. In the centre is a
skip, with a stool each side. The concert party is heard performing off.
Charles is finishing his face make-up in a hand mirror. Terri enters as
Miranda, tearing off his head-dress: during the following he changes into a
light suit with button-hole, as compère*

Terri Well, I've played some number three touring-dates in my time but
never anything to touch Kampong Uvula.

Charles I don't remember coming here with Tropic Scandals.

Terri Terri Dennis thanks Gillian Flack for a most enjoyable engagement
at His Majesty's, Tampon Kotex, with many happy memories of the
star dressing-room.

Charles And the lovely audiences.

Terri Oh don't! Not a single white face, just row upon row of brave little
Gurkhas. It's like staring at a pound of prunes.

Charles They say they never take out their kukris without drawing blood.

Terri I've always wanted to put that to the test.

Charles Oh, dear. Another double entendre.

Terri Hello.

Charles Well, there's nothing very funny about Gurkhas, is there? A race
of mercenary savages who'll fight for the British against their fellow-
Asians.

Terri My dear, is it your time of the month?

Charles Don't you ever tire of changing he to she or calling men by
women's names? There's nothing funny about being like this, either.

Terri Like what? Gay, you mean?

Charles *Queer.* What's gay about it? Most men like women, and most
women like men. We're queer, Terri, queer as coots. And I don't think
we should flaunt this cruel trick of nature. I think we should behave ourselves *more* than normal people. Your kind of promiscuity goes too far.
At your age you should be settling down. There.

Pause. Terri lights a cigarette and sits facing Charles

Terri And of course you're safe in the arms of Jessica.

Charles Sorry. Did it sound like that? My Salvationist background.

Terri You're safe for the time being but sooner or later you'll be on the
boat, leaving hubby on the Equator. England, nineteen forty-eight, is a
far cry from the Fleet Club, duckie. One lonely night you'll say a few
flattering words to some nice chap in a cottage and next you know a
cow of a magistrate's giving you three months.

Charles I'm not going home. I'm signing on to stay with Len. We've
sworn to stay with each other, whatever happens.

Terri Not going on the stage, then?

Charles Well, tell me honestly, d'you think I've got a chance?

Terri One must have talent or looks or preferably both. I was never Nijinsky, but I was a pretty face.

Charles And I'm not? (*He takes a "Flannagan" coat and hat from the skip*)

Terri The head in the middle's not bad.

Charles Thank you. So I suspected. (*Putting on the coat*) And as I'm no ornament I might as well be useful. I'm going back to male nursing.

Terri What about Len's wife?

Charles She's not bothered, there's plenty of what she wants at Aldershot.

Terri Len's a lucky man.

Charles I'm lucky, too.

Steve enters

Steve Come on, Charles, you're on.

Terri Thank your lucky stars you didn't fall for our new sergeant-major.

Steve Kevin's number's just finished.

Terri He'd have put you in the family way and left you for some suck-off-antics with the major.

Charles Any British turned up yet?

Steve Still out on patrol. Now get on.

Charles goes

Steve makes to follow

At the double!

Terri Wouldn't you? Duckie?

Steve What you on about?

Terri Oh, come on, Ada. Ever since you got the tiaras on the sleeve she never sees you.

Steve Who?

Terri *Who!* My dancing partner—the one you wanted to marry and take back to England. Or had you forgotten?

Steve The major said I should see a bit less of her for a while. Now I'm sergeant-major there's so much to do so little time

Terri You seem to spend most of it with him. What do you and the major get up to together? People are beginning to talk.

Steve We're reading *Pilgrim's Progress* together—*all* right!

Terri I'll tell Sylvia, it will be a great comfort to her.

Steve He seems to think she won't like life in England. Eurasian girls expect too much, he says. He may be right, Terri.

Terri Look, she's got a bun in the oven and *you* put it there. So when you're on that boat she'll be there too, or you'll answer to auntie. All right.

Steve I'm only trying to do my best by everyone.

Steve and Terri exit

A frontcloth comes down and the Lights change

SCENE 8

Pals

Charles and Len stroll on crooning a Flanagan-and-Allan kind of song. Len wears a suit and Charles the fur coat and straw hat

Charles ⎱ Though we've been far from Sunnyside Lane
Len   ⎰ You've never heard us complain
           But now that we're due in out of the rain
           We'll never leave it again.
           And once we've left those cloudy skies
           You'll hear us saying "Howdy, guys";
           Once Mister Blues is on the run
           You'll hear us greeting Mister Sun.
           Chorus
           Oh, we've been content
           Though we've never had a cent
           Because I've had you and you've had me,
           And every trouble and care
           Seemed so much less hard to bear
           'Cos we bore them in each other's company.

           Through all the storm-clouds we've been true
           To one another, just we two,
           But now the rainbow's in the blue,
           The sun will soon be shining through.

           And though we've too often strayed
           From the bright side to the shade,
           Together we shall never more roam
           From the heart of Home Sweet Home.

Charles and Len exit

The frontcloth goes up on the full stage, empty but bordered by dim jungle cut-outs. The lighting is bleak, from the front

SCENE 9

Even Their Relations Think They're Funny

Terri enters in a light suit as compère

Terri Thank you so much. Thank you for that nice little warm brown hand on our opening. So now you've seen a little of Costa Rica, we've brought you the heart-aches and joys of an Atlantic convoy and we've heard from one of the girls who's waiting for you at home. Well, not *you*, perhaps—anyway now Deception with a Difference brought to you by Love the Magician. Or for those of you who speak Spanish. *El Amor Brujo*. Not a titter. As a matter of interest, how many of you even speak English?

Giles (*from the audience*) *I* speak English.

Terri Well, screw *you* for a start.

Giles comes up on a corner of the stage

Giles Please watch your language, Mister Dennis.

Terri Oh, you! Then you're the only one who's got the faintest idea what we're on about. No wonder it's so quiet.

Giles They're enjoying it in their own way. They'll understand the conjuring. Carry on!

Terri Sir! Here she is then—Mean, Moody, Magnificent—Young-Love!

Eric comes on wearing a flowing gown and smoking a cigarette. He stares at Terri angrily: Terri goes

Eric does some passes, making his cigarette vanish, reappear, etc.

Eric The last time I did this trick was at Raffles Hotel, Singapore. I think. (*He takes a silver spoon from his pocket and looks at it*) Yes, Raffles Hotel. As a matter of fact, this isn't my usual line at all. I'm an operatic tenor. I was trained abroad. All the neighbours made a collection. My favourite song is the Milkmaid's Song: We must all pull together.

Giles Too much talk. Get on with it, man.

Eric Sir! This is known as the Russian Shuffle. Because, as you see, the cards are Russian from one end to the other. And now my Assistant, Miss Morgan, will show you that there is nothing in the cylinder.

Sylvia enters with a wand and magical props

Eric takes a cylinder from her and waves it with the magic wand

Completely empty. It's rather like a girl on a windy day. Now you see it, now you don't.

Giles No smut, thank you.

Eric No, sir. I give it two taps with the magic wand. Two taps—one hot, one cold—and hey presto . . .

All the Lights go out

Ah, now there appears to be a slight technical hitch.

Giles Oh dear! I'll go and have a look at the generator. I'll soon have it mended. Carry on conjuring.

Giles goes

Eric Hey presto, *voila!* I should perhaps explain that at this moment I am producing a variety of coloured handkerchiefs from the apparently empty cylinder. Hm. Er.

Pause

Sylvia The last time he did this trick . . .
Eric The last time I did this trick I had the audience in the palm of my hand. Which will give you some idea of the size of the audience.

There is the shriek of an animal in the jungle

Observe also that during this trick my hand never leaves the end of my arm. And there they are, all tied together. Thank you. And now my Assistant is going to come down amongst you for a volunteer . . .
Sylvia Don't be absurd, Eric! I wouldn't go near those fellows in the dark.

Terri enters

Terri Pack it in, love. I'll get the pianist to play something . . .

The Lights come on again. Eric is falling, with the props table—props are everywhere. Sylvia and others help him to clear them up. Terri comes down

And now may I have your attention for something a shade more serious?

The animal shrieks again

Thank you, Ada. A dramatic recitation.
"By the old Moulmein Pagoda looking eastward to sea
There's a Burma girl a-waiting and I know she thinks of me;
For the wind is in the palm-trees and the temple-bells . . ."

Kevin enters with a note

Kevin Excuse me.
Terri What? I'm trying to recite.
Kevin I've got an urgent police message.
Terri An urgent police message? Then read it this instant.
Kevin (*reading the note*) Will the person known as Pharoah last heard of two thousand years ago in Egypt, please go to the British Museum where his mummy's lying dangerously ill.
Terri Will you please get off the stage and permit me to continue. "For the wind is in the palm-trees . . ."

Kevin goes off. Steve comes on with a bucket

Where are you off to?
Steve To see my brother.
Terri Where is he?
Steve He's in jail.
Terri What's the bucket for?
Steve To bail him out.

Steve goes

Terri I'm trying to give these little brown gentlemen a recitation.
"Come you back, you British soldier, come you back to Mandalay . . ."

Len enters with a bucket, wearing a crinoline and a wig

Where are you going?

Len To milk a cow.
Terri In that wig?
Len No, in this bucket.

Len goes, spilling water from the bucket

Terri Kindly leave the upturned tea-chests.
"For the wind is in the palm-trees and the temple-bells they say . . ."

Kevin enters with a bottle

Kevin Bottle of truth, bottle of truth!
Terri What's that?
Kevin One drink of this and you must tell the truth!
Terri Let me try that. (*He drinks*) It's paraffin!
Kevin That's the truth!

Charles comes on as Kevin goes off

Terri "And the temple bells they say . . ."
Charles Excuse me . . .
Terri Excuse me, British soldier—no! D'you mind? I'm trying to recite poetry.
Charles Poetry? Ah, poetry!
"The dog stood on the burning deck, The flames were leaping round his neck—hot dog!"

Charles goes

Terri (*desperately*) "Come you back, you British soldier . . ."

Kevin enters

Kevin Where's the major?
Terri Where's the major? I don't know, where *is* . . .
Kevin They're attacking the camp . . .
Terri I'm attempting to recite Kipling . . .
Kevin They're inside, I've seen them . . .
Terri I don't remember this, duckie, what's the . . .

Len runs on, wearing the crinoline

Len They've knifed the fucking guard, the fucking Commies.

Len turns to shout at the audience

Lee and Cheng come on upstage with sten guns

Bandit shoot Gurkha chowkidar . . .
Kevin Oh!

All the Lights go out, and in the darkness Lee and Cheng fire rapid bursts towards the audience. Cries of alarm and pain from everyone onstage

Steve Sylvia!

Steve and Sylvia find each other through the carnage and embrace, looking at their friends, groaning on the floor

The Lights come up, to show all the Company on stage. Len is lying dead. Kevin is crying out and lying on the ground. Terri is also on the ground, with Charles binding up his leg. Sylvia and Steve are nursing Kevin, and Eric moves about with buckets

Giles enters downstage and speaks to the audience

As Giles speaks the Lights gradually fade to a spot on him and a faint light on Len's body

Giles (*as he enters*) Right. Thank you. So? Was I right? Had it been good thinking? Yes is the answer—and sucks to the desk-wallahs at G.H.Q. I sensed as soon as the lights went out that my little plan was beginning to bear fruit. I made for the generator and sure enough found that the juice had been switched off. So that when I turned the lights on, imagine the terrorists' consternation at being faced by row upon row of un-smiling Mongol faces watching a British comedy show. moreover, a show performed by highly trained jungle fighters. This was indeed a Parade of Privates they had not anticipated. At any rate they panicked and let off bursts of rapid fire into the midst of them. Now that was very bad thinking because Johnny Gurkha doesn't stand arguing the toss, it's out with his kukri and off with their heads. The terrorist got a total bag of four: three Gurkhas and one B.O.R. Making a final score of six–four to us. I was sorry to lose poor Bonny. He was one of the best. Not perhaps bursting with imagination but steady, loyal, dependable. After being brought up in the sewers of Birmingham, the darkness and filth of the jungle held no terrors for him. And if you'd praised him for playing his part in the defence of freedom, he might well have protested, "Lor' bless my soul, sir, that's a load of 'umbug and no error . . ."

Charles comes down to Len and kneels beside him

A particularly tragic aspect of his death is that I'd recently arranged—without his knowledge—to have his wife posted out to join him. This was to have been a pleasant surprise on our return to Singapore.

Charles kisses Len's face

Alas, this happy reunion was not to be. And as he went he said, "Death, where is thy sting?" And as he went down deeper he said, "Grave where is thy victory?" So he passed over and all the trumpets sounded for him on the other side.

Giles goes

The Lights fade to a Black-out

SCENE 10

Finale: Bless 'em All

The Lights come up full to reveal a backcloth of a large ship, with a gangway leading up to it. Charles enters, pushing Kevin in a wheelchair

Kevin There she is, Charlie. The boat. We made it.

Charles stops and brakes the chair

Charles Some of us.

Kevin After a fashion.

Charles There is some corner of a foreign field that is forever fucking England.

Kevin I'm glad to see it, all the same. Glad to be going home and all, even though I'll never know what it's like to have a white bint. I mean, it was all in a good cause. We kept the old flag flying, eh? Helped save a bit of the Empire from the Chinese, eh?

Charles Having brought them here in the first place to work our tin-mines.

Kevin We may be a tiny little island, Charlie, but no-one pushes us about.

Charles My dear, keeping rubber for democracy won't give you back your balls. Or Len his life. What odds would it make to Len whether England was Communist, Fascist, or Anabaptist? He'd still be working in a stores somewhere, making lists, getting what he could out of life . . .

Kevin I reckon if he could speak to us now . . .

Charles He can't though, can he? He never could. Born in a dump in Smethwick that's not one of the things you learn.

Eric comes in from the same way

Eric Come along then, juldi, juldi, what are we waiting for?

Kevin The Old Man. We've all got to assemble on the dock, he wants to say a few words.

Charles Tell me when he doesn't.

Eric Sooner we get mobile sooner I'll be home to sort out creepie-crawlie Roy Lawrence of the Flying Feet. He'll dance to another tune, believe me. (*He shoots out his wrist to look at his watch, takes out his cigarette case, gives Kevin one and takes one himself*)

Charles What good's a bunch of fives going to do? They're engaged.

Eric Then they can ruddy well get disengaged, my old mucker. At the double! (*He tries in vain to work his lighter*)

Charles Face facts . . .

Eric Facts? The facts are Susan's my girl and he's pushed in. The facts are—(*he gives up trying to work the lighter*)—I hope this is the last I see of damned cheapjack Chinese rubbish!

Kevin supplies a match

Steve and Sylvia are driven on in a trishaw by Lee. She is beginning to show her pregnancy and is prettily dressed as for a garden party. Steve is uniformed, but has one arm in a sling and splint

Sylvia Hallo, boys, better late than never!
Steve Where's the Old Man?
Kevin No sign yet.

Steve helps Sylvia down. Lee begins unloading her hand-baggage for the voyage. Steve comes down to speak to the audience

Steve Dear Everyone at Fifty-Six, this is the last you'll hear before the boat. Five weeks' time I'll be with you all, by which time my arm should be almost mended.

The other men laugh and talk to Sylvia

Thank you for getting my old room ready but can you fit in a *double*-bed because my wife Sylvia will be coming with me! She is half-Indian, half-Welsh and I'm quite sure you will all make her feel at home because she is so looking forward to meeting you and her grandma who lives in Swansea.

Sylvia joins Steve

Sylvia Don't forget to tell them I'm pregnant.
Steve And here's another surprise: within a few months you'll be grandparents. Sorry not to have told you sooner but with all that trouble in the jungle it slipped my mind. So you see, Dad, the army *has* made a man of me, though rather late in the day. See you soon, don't write any more . . .
Sylvia Sylvia sends her love.
Steve And so do I. Steve.

They go upstage. Steve pays Lee

Lee drives off

Sylvia looks about anxiously

Voice on Speaker Attention, please, attention, please. All British Other Ranks are now embarking at Godown Forty-two. Hurry it up, there.

The ship's horn sounds

Sylvia Where's the major got to?
Steve Stop panicking.
Sylvia I'm like a cat on hot bricks. Nearly thirty years I've been waiting for this day but Mummy always said, "There's many a slip twixt the cup and the lip", and no-one knew better than she.
Steve You native women are all the same: riddled with superstition. (*He kisses her*)

Terri enters, walking with sticks to support an injured leg. With him, in the uniform of the Civil Police, is Cheng carrying a suitcase, which he puts down

Terri This is an outrage! I've never been so insulted throughout the whole of my professional career.

Charles Not another drama?

Terri Drama! I've given my all for the boys and my reward is being rushed to the boat as though I'd got the Black Death. I keep telling this officer I have no political convictions but look at her! The Laughing Policewoman!

Sylvia You've been misbehaving again.

Terri Talk about the pot calling the kettle. My dear!

Steve What happened?

Terri I got discharged from hospital yesterday and spent the day quietly with friends. Late at night I arrived back at Raffles with this sweet little matelot, hobbled up to my room and let him in without switching on the lights. He was all over me before I could draw breath. "Oo, sir, you're a smasher, ooo, sir, you're a dream." I asked him could he possibly forget I was an officer, just for the time being but it's strange how many of them like all that, the suck-off antics, so I let him rave on. "Oh, Captain, let me give you a baby" and so on till he had to run and catch the liberty boat. I waved good-bye from the balcony and was back in the dark room lighting myself a soothing Churchman's when suddenly a voice whispered in the darkness "Could you oblige me with a light?"

Sylvia Oh, Terri! Where from?

Terri The other bed.

Charles Oh no!

Terri Well, there'd always been two in there, as you know, and I suppose in my absence they'd filled the other. With the net pulled down I hadn't noticed.

Charles Who was it?

Terri Some old duck.

Sylvia What did he say?

Terri Nothing more. I offered her a light and she said "Thank you" and that was the last I heard till this morning when the manager told me I'd be escorted to the docks and put on the next boat home.

Charles So the man in the bed had shopped you?

Terri Well, there's some would sell their mother for a cream slice.

Kevin But you were going on this boat anyway!

Terri That's not the point. Is this any way to treat a celebrated war heroine? Someone who's made the sacrifices I've made! I shan't let it rest, believe me. You'll be hearing from my member.

Voice on Speaker All visitors ashore now, please, all visitors ashore.

Eric Let's get on board, Chief.

Sylvia Oh yes, darling, please, let's not miss the boat after all this time.

Steve All right, everyone, you get on board, I'll wait for the Old Man— Company, commanding officer on parade. Company—'shun!

Giles comes on from the side, with Lee carrying his personal luggage. Lee exits up the gangplank

Giles (*saluting*) Stand easy. Well, everyone, we shall certainly meet again during the five weeks at sea, but as fellow-passengers, not comrades-in-arms. So I want to take this last opportunity of inviting you to drop in for tea if you find yourself in Berkshire. Nothing remarkable, of course, only a simple seventeenth-century mill-house, typical of hundreds throughout the length and breadth of England. No very brilliant company either—only my wife and the Labradors. (*He addresses much of this to Steve*) Perhaps a spot of hunting, freshwater fishing. If any of you is a rubber there's a fine Jacobean brass in the Norman church. In other words, the ordinary everyday England we've been striving to save. Worth fighting for. Worth dying for. For whether he chooses a humble cottage, a great house or only a bamboo hovel in a jungle clearing, every soldier dreams of the day when he can say—as we say now . . .

Giles leads everyone into a reprise of the Home-Sweet-Home song

All   We're going back
To that homely little shack
On the sunny side of any street.
We've been too long
From the laughter and the song
That we'll share with all the folks we're going to meet.

I know a lady living there
With shining eyes and silver hair
And when she offers me a chair
I'm going to feel a millionaire.

So though we've travelled around
Now's the time to settle down
And when we're there we'll never more roam
From the heart of Home-Sweet-Home.

After the first reprise of the song Giles shakes hands with the Company while the music continues

Lee returns empty-handed, and Giles gives him money

Terri (*during the reprise of the music*)
In fairyland, my dears, there's nothing new—
True love, a song, a dance, a death or two.
I've done my best to keep the party clean;
If we've offended, blame the poor old queen.
All fairies have the gift of prophecy,
So here's my hint of what is yet to be:
In ten years' time we'll win Malaya's war
Then once again surrender Singapore.
And as for what Dame Fate's got up her sleeve

For Giles, Charles, Kevin, Eric, Sylvia, Steve . . .
But no! Since at the start I promised laughter
Let's say: They all lived happy ever after.

The line reforms as they follow Giles towards the gangplank in the following order: Steve, Sylvia, Eric, Kevin, Charles, Terri

All   So though we've travelled around
Now it's time to settle down
And when we're there we'll never more stray
From the Paradise that's sunny all day,
Which is why we're sailing over the foam
To the heart of Home-Sweet-Home.

As they move across, the men wave to the audience. Lee and Cheng remain on stage level, waving at them, as

the CURTAIN *falls*

CURTAIN CALL

All   You may as well surrender when you hear our battle cry
There'll be no more escaping when we raise our weapons high.
And in the vict'ry cavalcade
you'll see the Privates on Parade
On Parade—Parade!

FURNITURE AND PROPERTY LIST

ACT I
SCENE 1

Nil

SCENE 2

Nil

SCENE 3

On stage: Bar counter. *On it:* various drinks including beer, gin, orangeade assorted glasses, glass-polisher
2 small tables
4 chairs

SCENE 4

On stage: Bentwood chair (on inner stage)

SCENE 5

On stage: Dressing-table with lighted mirror. *On it:* bottle of gin, 2 glasses, various items of theatrical make-up, towel, cigarettes, matches
Dress rack with **Terri**'s costumes
2 chairs

SCENE 6

Nil

SCENE 7

On stage: Dressing-table with mirror. *On it:* various items of theatrical make-up, cigarettes, matches
Sylvia's dress rack
2 chairs
Small bamboo table. *On it:* portable wind-up gramophone with record of *An English Country Garden* in place

SCENE 8

On stage: Small desk. *On it:* candle, pen, paper
Movable stand microphone
Shower unit (set when tabs close after **Terri** leaves desk)

SCENE 9

On stage: Bed and bedding
Wicker chair
Tin-trunk. *On it:* 2 top hats, 2 canes
Small table. *On it:* gramophone from Scene 7
Sylvia's clothes on rack or pegs

SCENE 10

On stage: Tree-stump

SCENE 11

On stage: Mound of earth by grave trap

SCENE 12

As SCENE 9

On stage: *On tin-trunk:* tray with teapot, 2 cups, 2 saucers
On gramophone: record of *Greensleeves*

Off stage: Kit-bag **(Steve)**
Clipboard and papers **(Len)**
Skip. *In it:* tights, brassière, wigs, dressing **(Len)**
Various kit items, including stripes, cap, badges, patent shoes **(Len)**
Cardboard box with make-up items **(Len)**
7 lettered parasols, forming S.A.D.U.S.E.A. **(Cast)**
Case of beer **(Cheng)**
Bottle of lotion **(Cheng)**
Large cylinder of lemonade crystals **(Eric)**
5 letters: one, for **Eric**, containing shapshot **(Len)**
Tray with 5 glasses of beer **(Cheng)**
2 glasses of lemonade **(Cheng)**
Revolver and bullets **(Cheng)**
Rifle with fixed bayonet **(Steve)**
Letter **(Steve)**
Torch **(Steve)**
Whistle **(Steve)**
2 shovels **(Lee, Cheng)**
Coffin with Union Jack **(Bearers)**
Sword **(Giles)**
Loaded rifle **(Len)**

Personal: **Steve:** box of matches, chit, towel
Terri: cigarette in holder
Eric: spectacles, handkerchief, penknife, towel
Reg: cane, pen, handkerchief
Sylvia: watch
Kevin: towel
Charles: towel
Len: towel

ACT II
SCENE 1

On stage: Table. *On it:* champagne in bucket, champagne glass

SCENE 2

On stage: Desk. *On it:* writing-materials, papers, folders, teapot, cup, saucer
2 chairs
On wall: map of Malaya, photo of George VI

Scene 3

Nil

SCENE 4

Nil

SCENE 5

On stage: Train carriage with 2 compartments, tables between wooden benches,
kit-bags on racks
In one compartment: pack of cards, "swear money" tin, cigarettes,
matches

SCENE 6

Nil

SCENE 7

On stage: Skip. *In it:* **Terri**'s compère suit, **Charles**'s "Flanagan" coat and hat,
make-up items, hand-mirror
2 stools

SCENE 8

Nil

SCENE 9

On stage: Jungle cut-out borders around bare stage

SCENE 10

On stage: Gangway leading into ship

Off stage: Teacup and saucer **(Cheng)**
Trishaw **(Lee)**
7 rifles **(Squad** and **Sylvia)**
Letter, for **Eric (Len)**
Silver spoon **(Eric)**
Small table with "magic" props, including wand and cylinder **(Sylvia)**
Note **(Kevin)**
Bucket **(Steve)**
Bucket with water **(Len)**
Bottle **(Kevin)**
2 sten guns **(Lee, Cheng)**
Wheel-chair **(Kevin)**
Sling, splint **(Steve)**
Hand luggage **(Sylvia)**
Sticks or crutch **(Terri)**
Suitcase **(Cheng)**
Giles's personal luggage **(Lee)**

Personal: **Giles:** keys, coins
Len: coins, wallet with photograph
Eric: wristwatch, empty cigarette-case, lighter, cigarette for conjuring
scene
Kevin: box of matches
Steve: coins

LIGHTING PLOT

Property fittings required: set of mirror bulbs
Numerous small sets on open stage, interior and exterior

ACT I

To open:	Black-out	
Cue 1	**Steve** starts to leave *Overhead light switched on*	(Page 1)
Cue 2	**Chorus:** "All ready." *House Lights up*	(Page 4)
Cue 3	**Terri:** ". . . your working lights." *Overhead light switched on*	(Page 4)
Cue 4	**Terri:** ". . . your house lights." *Black-out*	(Page 4)
Cue 5	**Len:** "Fucking thing!" *Overhead lights up*	(Page 4)
Cue 6	Band strikes up *Full lighting for opening song*	(Page 6)
Cue 7	At end of song *Change to bar lighting*	(Page 7)
Cue 8	**Steve:** "Don't we all!" *Cross-fade to lighting for "Movie" song*	(Page 11)
Cue 9	**Terri:** "*Auf Wiedersehen.*" *Fade to Black-out, then spot on* **Steve**	(Page 12)
Cue 10	**Reg** exits *Cross-fade to lighting on dressing-room scene, with mirror bulbs*	(Page 12)
Cue 11	**Terri** turns to audience *Fade to spot on* **Terri**	(Page 16)
Cue 12	**Terri** exits *Bring up lighting for Western Approaches ballet—spot on* **Sylvia**, *then up to half-light with dramatic flashes*	(Page 16)
Cue 13	Music stops *Bring up lighting to full*	(Page 17)
Cue 14	On general exit *Fade to spot on* **Terri**	(Page 20)
Cue 15	**Terri:** ". . . wherefore art thou, matelot?" *Bring up general lighting on* **Sylvia's** *dressing-room*	(Page 20)
Cue 16	**Sylvia** switches out lights *Snap off lights in dressing-room*	(Page 23)

Cue 17	**Steve** exits	(Page 24)
	Bring up spots on **Terri** *at desk*	
Cue 18	**All:** "But we'll do them for ever more." (song ends)	(Page 25)
	Cross-fade to bright lighting on showers	
Cue 19	**Giles** exits	(Page 30)
	Fade to spot on **Reg**	
Cue 20	**Reg:** ". . . Special Investigation Branch."	(Page 30)
	Cross-fade to special torch lighting for "Greensleeves" song	
Cue 21	During third verse of song	(Page 31)
	Bring up dim lighting on **Sylvia's** *room*	
Cue 22	As song ends	(Page 31)
	Bring up lighting to full	
Cue 23	At end of SCENE 9	(Page 33)
	Reduce to front lighting	
Cue 24	**Cheng** and **Lee** exit	(Page 34)
	Black-out—then dim, stormy light, lightning flashes	
Cue 25	**Eric** and **Steve** carry **Reg** off	(Page 35)
	Black-out, then up to full stage lighting	
Cue 26	At end of funeral	(Page 36)
	Fade to spots on **Giles** *and* **Company**	
Cue 27	General exit at end of song	(Page 37)
	Bring up full lighting on **Sylvia's** *room*	
Cue 28	**Sylvia:** "Now come to bed . . ."	(Page 40)
	Fade to spot on **Steve**	

ACT II

To open:	Front lighting full up	
Cue 29	**Terri** exits	(Page 42)
	Bring up lighting on office	
Cue 30	**Giles** exits	(Page 46)
	Fade to overall night lighting	
Cue 31	Trishaw is taken off	(Page 47)
	Cross-fade to bright daylight	
Cue 32	General exit after song	(Page 51)
	Cross-fade to train scene, with light concentrated on carriage: flashing lights	
Cue 33	**Giles** enters	(Page 54)
	Cross-fade to spot on **Giles**	
Cue 34	**Giles** exits	(Page 55)
	Bring up spots on **Terri** *for "Miranda" song*	
Cue 35	**Terri:** "The Latin-American Way." (second verse)	(Page 55)
	Bring up overhead lighting	
Cue 36	**Steve** and **Terri** exit	(Page 57)
	Bring up spot on **Charles** *and* **Len**	

EFFECTS PLOT

ACT I

Cue 1 As men go to shower cubicles (Pages 26–27)
Sound of running water: stop as last man comes out

Cue 2 **Steve:** ". . . she was in a club." (Page 32)
Westminster Chimes sound six o'clock

Cue 3 **Lee** and **Cheng** exit (Page 34)
*Sound of heavy rain, thunder, nocturnal animals: continue
through scene*

ACT II

Cue 4 At start of train scene (Page 51)
Sound of steam train, wheels, clouds of steam

Cue 5 **Eric:** ". . . size of the audience." (Page 60)
Shriek of jungle animal

Cue 6 **Terri:** ". . . a shade more serious?" (Page 60)
Animal shriek

Cue 7 Lights go out after **Lee** and **Cheng** enter with guns (Page 61)
Loud bursts of rapid fire

Cue 8 **Loud-Speaker Voice:** "Hurry it up, there." (Page 64)
Ship's horn sounds

MADE AND PRINTED IN GREAT BRITAIN BY
LATIMER TREND & COMPANY LTD PLYMOUTH

MADE IN ENGLAND